BOWIEODYSSEY71

Also by Simon Goddard

Bowie Odyssey 70
The Comeback
Rollaresque
Simply Thrilled
Ziggyology
Mozipedia
Songs That Saved Your Life

BOWIE**ODYSSEY**71

SIMON**GODDARD**

OMNIBUS PRESS

London / New York / Paris / Sydney / Copenhagen / Berlin / Madrid / Tokyo

Note to the Reader: The following narrative takes place in 1971 and contains language and prevailing attitudes of the time which some readers may find offensive. The publishers wish to reassure that all such instances are there specifically for reasons of historical social context in order to accurately describe the period concerned.

TO LEESA
Alexandra Maternity Home, 1971

BOWIECONTENTS71

'Every day it becomes more apparent that people are not going to take the shit that's coming down! People are organising everywhere – the shipbuilders are running Clydeside, the people of Ireland are fighting for their self-determination, women are fighting back a male-ego-chauvinist world and our black brothers and sisters are fighting the racism of a white-dominated world. And now, also, homosexuals are standing up and saying, "No more shit!" Our oppression ends here.'

GAY LIBERATION FRONT YOUTH GROUP,
SPEAKERS' CORNER, HYDE PARK,
LONDON, 28 AUGUST 1971

ONE

'Is that David Bowie?'

THE BELLE OF THE BALL ASKS PRINCE CHARMING, her lips so close her breath tickles his ear. It's the only way she can be sure he'll hear her above the booming *buh-buh-buh-buh* of The Jackson 5. Beneath their feet flashes an aurora borealis of reds and greens as the lights under the crowded coloured Perspex dancefloor flicker to the bubbling beat, though these two would cast a limelight strong enough without it. She is a starlet: Hollywood by way of Chelsea, Terry de Havilland heels spreading the gospel of glitz with every tread. So is he: a blond Nureyev in a home-sewn ballet of jacket and culottes, every stitch flattering his lithe physique like cotton applause. They come not merely to dance, but to dazzle. And they do.

'OH MY GAAAD!'

Not two minutes ago a new admirer blew up in their faces like a Texas oil gusher.

'YOU TWO LOOK *FAAABULOUS!*'

An invitation followed.

'COME OVER AND SIT WITH US AND HAVE SOME CHAMPAAAGNE!'

The messenger then sashayed back to one of the red velvet booths surrounding the dancefloor occupied by the other half of 'US' – a long-haired creature in something like a dress. It was the girl who recognised

1

the face beneath its fringe: the same cute face that sang the song she loved a year or so ago about the loneliness of space. But where that head used to be covered in short blond curls, this one has hair like Rapunzel. That's why she had to ask her friend: 'Is *that* David Bowie?'

IT IS. David Bowie, known for 'Space Oddity' and nothing else, sits in a salmon-pink floral gown enveloped by the velvet upholstery, legs crossed and skirted, one hand absently toying with the stem of a glass as he stares across the rainbow ripple of bumping bodies. On the table in front of him sighs a plate of limp lettuce and jaundiced ham, deposited ten minutes earlier by a blur of a waiter in dungarees by Mr Freedom. David, frocked by Mr Fish, doesn't touch it. Identical plates wilt undisturbed in the adjacent booths, compliments of the management who include a 'snack supper' in the price of entry to satisfy late licensing laws. The salad is purely superficial. So are the clientele. The men from the magazine that once was *Jeremy* came, saw and catclawed scathing judgement a year ago. *'Here the ultimate is cool. Fashion. Poise. The trendy dolly set where the impression is that if any of the boys, or girls, have sex it's in front of their bedroom mirror – on their own.'* The trendy dolly set sum it up in a single phrase: 'piss-elegant'. It's the only style that counts in the Sombrero.

Nothing here being what it seems, 'the Sombrero' isn't really the Sombrero. The club's proper name, as its silver matchbooks remind, is Yours Or Mine? The actual Sombrero – *El Sombrero* – is the Mexican restaurant above it on Kensington High Street at the corner of Campden Hill Road. *'Eees good!'* swears the advert. *'Eees very good!'* El Sombrero is unmissable on account of the neon sombrero mounted outside which lights up at night beside the ground-level entrance to the club in its basement. Both are owned by the same little Swiss man called Harry who opened the Sombrero as a café in the Fifties, choosing the name because he liked holidaying in Spain. When it burned down in the Sixties he rebuilt it, enlarging the cellar into a nightclub, the first in London with an illuminated dancefloor, which he brought over from Switzerland. Dining above or dancing below, it's all 'the Sombrero'.

The unruly queue to what nobody calls Yours Or Mine? snakes along the front of the restaurant, waiting to reach the foyer beyond the neon hat.

Once past two butch Yugoslavian doormen and the cherubic cloakroom boy, it's down the stairs to be greeted by the flamboyant manager, Amadeo, a sweep of blond hair and a Noël Coward cigarette holder clenched between his large teeth, removed only to welcome his regulars with a three-syllable *'dha-rrr-ling!'* A podium waits beyond the bottom step, lure to a steady pageant of Glorias out-Swansoning one another as they make their entrance. Only when they've posed long enough to be seen by all – tossing a wrist, batting an eyelid or tilting a chin in imaginary close-up – have they finally *arrived*.

Some of these lives are penny-poor, but their chic remains priceless. Many are gimcrack Cinderellas, underpaid boutique assistants taking the merchandise they sell but can never afford out on the tiles for a midnight twirl before hanging it back on the rails to be sold on as factory-fresh Yves Saint Laurent. Even the most destitute boast the apparel of rich imagination: a bedsheet becomes a toga and a cheap plastic crown of laurel leaves painted gold makes a daytime nobody a disco Nero. No awkward questions are asked. Everyone is taken at face value and nothing here has more value than face. It is a place to be what you wish, not what you are. King's Road queens, Mandraxed coquettes, hustlers, dandies, fops, tarts, gigolos and speed freaks. All damned, but in the glow of the Sombrero, all damned beautiful.

The most beautiful never go on Saturdays, the air too soured by the hick perfume of awayday amateurs. Better are odd nights midweek and best of all Sunday, the in-est in-crowd's favourite, when those who come to sparkle and be envied sparkle brightest and are envied greenest. The ones who never queue, never pay and who, when not dancing, blow pearls of Polari slang between cigarette puffs in the DJ booth with Antonello, a handsome, dry-witted Italian hairdresser who supplies the sounds to keep the black bombers ticking till 3 a.m. Ones like the glittering Fred and Ginger currently stealing glances at the homi-polone they think might be the one-hit-wonder David Bowie.

Fred is a Freddie, but Ginger is a Wendy – a streetwise Fulham girl, slender, attractive and naked if not in Quorum, Biba or similarly swish fabric. Most days she sleeps long past noon after working nights as a hostess at Churchill's on New Bond Street, her job to flatter its wealthy gentlemen into leaving the premises several hundred pounds poorer on a bellyful of champagne and caviar. Few can resist Wendy's allure. Freddie is six foot, fair of hair with eyes of blue, registered with a model agency though the main benefactors of his pulchritude are a rougher sort of trade. First and fashionmost he is a tailor, for now employed taking in alterations on the King's Road but conserving his full talent for the private industry of the little sewing machine he uses like an indispensable fifth limb. He is an entirely self-stitched creation, even his name, 'Freddie Burretti', a necessary Italianate embroidering of Bletchley's Fred Burrett. His wardrobe is his world and the world a catwalk to exhibit his wardrobe, complemented, always, by black lace-up shoes with thick cork soles.

Together, they rent a flat in Holland Park, more threadbare than the location suggests save for an Aubrey Beardsley print on the wall as a concession to class. There are two bedrooms: one a double where they sleep together, though not as lovers, the other spare for Freddie's occasional assignations. Two black sheep cast out from their families who've since found sibling love in one another, neither are yet 20 years old. Freddie is brother and domestic mother, Wendy the little sister alien to the use of a dishcloth, too busy waiting for the next rap on the door from 'Fifi' and his hoisting gang bearing dresses shoplifted to order from the pages of the latest *Vogue*. You'll sometimes see Freddie and Wendy in Chelsea, down La Douce in Soho, or over in Earl's Court at the Catacombs or the Boston – wherever the straight grey world of Courtelle-sweater Janets and their Hai Karate Johns never interferes. The same reason they love the Sombrero best of all.

IT IS ANGIE, David's wife, who first hears about the Sombrero, and it is Angie who persuades him they should go. He doesn't resist. She'd been tipped off by one of the gals in Al Parker's, the West End theatrical agency where she'd been temping to bring in some extra cash. But if they hadn't told her, sooner or later somebody else would have. The Sombrero was much too Angie a kind of place to hide its whereabouts from her for very long: wild fashion, hot disco and packed with more queers than a plainclothes policeman can shake his stick at. Within seconds of arrival, it is already everything they said it would be, and more.

David is quick to gauge the piss-elegant climate and fixes his mask accordingly. But inside his heart skips. In his long tresses and floral print dress he realises he is no longer the most fascinating creature in the room. Nor the most androgynous. David spots Freddie dancing with Wendy in his first sensory-overloaded blink like the optical ringing of an orchestra chime. He sees handsome, stylish, pretentious; a peacock, an actor, an incorrigible poser; a lost boy, much like himself. David needs to have his curiosity satisfied but is unused to making first moves unaided. That's why Angie is here.

'OH! AREN'T . . . THEY. . . *FAAABULOUS!*'

David dispatches Angie to cross the dancefloor and lure them to their booth. The scene flickers before him like a silent movie. Angie confidently approaching, eyes glowing, arm pointing, the girl and the boy flashing their eyes over in his direction, nervous smiles, mouths moving, their every word a mystery buried beneath the lovelorn holler of little Michael Jackson.

Angie returns alone.

'THEY'RE COMING OVER.'

Freddie and Wendy are still holding conference. Freddie decides she's right. It *is* David Bowie.

'What do you think?' asks Wendy. 'Should we go over?'

Skipping to a stranger's table at the first sniff of champagne isn't the piss-elegant thing to do. Instinct says no. But intrigue says yes. Freddie purses his lips. Then a smirk. 'Come on, then.'

The dancefloor blinks blue as the tempo changes to the African boogie of Miriam Makeba's 'Pata Pata'. Angie's radiating smile claps to their cool approach as two become four. Necessary introductions. 'Wendy.' 'ANGIE.' 'Freddie.' 'David,' says David, and his guests nod like they don't already know. The light is soft but clear enough for mutual close inspection. Freddie is fascinated by David's skew-pupilled eyes, one gleaming infinitely bluer than the other. David calculates Freddie's hair, lips and cheekbones and decides he looks a lot like Mick Jagger: possibly the *next* Mick Jagger.

'Do you sing?' asks David.

'I used to be in the school choir,' says Freddie with a coy flutter. 'But that was before my voice broke. I really had a very good voice before.

5

Like *most* young boys.' His eyes dapple with mischief. 'No,' he continues, 'I design clothes. I make all my own.' He gently pinches his lapel. 'I made this.'

David twitches an eyebrow. 'Could you make something for me?'

Freddie's gaze drops down to David's navel and back up again. 'I could.' He raises his glass to his lips and takes a long, delicate sip. 'If you give me your measurements.'

David smiles. Wendy giggles. Angie howls.

'OH, DARLING! PLEASE, YOU *MUST* MAKE DAVID SOMETHING FAAABULOUS!'

More bubbles are poured, infinities of unspoken kinships noted. By the bottom of the bottle an alliance of *enfants terribles* is forged. They talk, they drink, they dance; all the while David and Freddie softly scrutinise one another, each an artist beginning to sense that the search for their next muse is over.

Numbers and vows to reconvene again are exchanged. Their first visit to the Sombrero will not be David and Angie's last; by the earliest blossom of spring they will be as much a part of its fabric as red velvet, rent boys and 'Lay Down' by Melanie, Antonello's habitual four-minute warning that the party's over. For some it continues, Freddie and Wendy taking their appetites down the road to a Persian café with the rest of their pep-pilled dawn chorus. But not for David and Angie, who totter into a taxi, Beckenham-bound, minds kaleidoscoping in blissful aftershock as they slump down in the backseat. Their bodies rock to the soft rhythm of the road, his hand on her knee as his eyes begin to droop. Hers follow. Then suddenly snap wide open.

'OH!'

Pinprick-sized ears formed from cells not grown a week ago to hear the thump of Melanie are tingling with new sensation. She gasps again, louder, and David stirs from his Jagger-faced dream. Angie places his hand on her tummy.

'Can you *feel*?'

Beneath the skin, tiny legs are dancing.

TWO

JAGGER-FACED DREAMS turn to terror on a 43-foot screen. The film, *Performance*, stars the Rolling Stone as Turner, a rock star recluse, abandoned by his demon, sectioning himself to a claustrophobic bedlam of psychotropic orgies with his two girlfriends in a Notting Hill townhouse. A suspicious interloper moves in downstairs, a bruised James Fox with slicked-back hair, crudely dyed the colour of red–hot-red. He says he's a juggler, 'Johnny Dean', but Jagger doesn't believe him, nor should he. Fox is really a gangster named Chas: a shooter, a whipper, a wrecker of Rollers with battery acid, a general putter of frighteners on flash little twerps, he's now on the run from his own firm after killing an acquaintance. His last salvation, this bohemian 'pisshole' in Powis Square.

'If you were me, what would you do?' asks Jagger.

'It depends who you are,' answers Fox, and in the blink of a bisexual trip the pop idol and the mobster slowly realise they are one and the same – each only a performer of the character they think they see staring back at themselves in the mirror.

As its poster says, it's a film about 'MADNESS AND SANITY, FANTASY AND REALITY, DEATH AND LIFE, VICE AND VERSA'. The hippie press are calling it *'the heaviest movie ever made'*, which explains why it's been gathering dust for two years on the censor's shelf, awaiting the queasy snips only now allowing it to receive its charity premiere at the Warner West End four days before David's 24th birthday. The first red carpet of 1971 sees a bleary parade of rock musicians, actors, disc jockeys and models, but no Mick Jagger. He's stranded at a Parisian airport at the mercy of Janvier fog. As a second best, Keith Richards drains the Fleet Street flashbulbs, arm in arm with his partner and the film's co-star Anita Pallenberg, about to be seen in an hour's time rolling starkers under a bedsheet with Keith's best mate in glorious Technicolor.

David's face is not famous enough for the premiere but in his first lungful of turning 24 he winds through Leicester Square to see it for himself. Only to *see* himself. His colourless London of Portobello litter and ciggie-stinking phone boxes on Wandsworth Bridge Road. His fortress flat of paintbox walls, guitars and speakers, rails of strange clothes, freaky antiques and exotic rugs. His and Angie's bed jumping with women kissing men who may be women kissing women who may be men. His voice when lips move and say, 'I'm 'avin' a laugh, you see, with my image.' He is Turner of Beckenham, freecloud poet. 'I want to empty my skull, completely.' He is Chas of Brixton, cocky little wide boy. 'I like a bit of a cavort.' One and both, vice and versa, Jones and Bowie.

'The only performance that makes it, that really makes it, that makes it all the way, is the one that achieves madness. Right?'

The die is cast, in red-hot-red.

Performance blows David's mind.

THE BOY CALLED MARK FROM WALNUT COURT, the block of flats across the road from David, sits listening to him evangelise about *Performance*. Evangelise is the only way to describe it. David doesn't talk about it like someone who's seen a film but someone who's seen the light. He radiates it in 100-watt words flickering between cigarette puffs, eyes bright as 70mm projector bulbs. Clearly possessed, but just as clearly inspired. In the white-hot filament of his brain, ideas now blaze in Sombrero dancefloor reds and yellows, waking him up in the dead of night, eyelids dynamited open by mad words and wild music. They are gifts from the gods of slumber, scattering phantoms at 4 a.m. as he stumbles in moonlit gloom to the nearest pen, pad and instrument to ignite the glowing embers before they cool and die, dawn driving away ghoul-at-the-window nightmares as tunes rattle out of his head in gentle sharps and unexpected sixths. He shocks himself with his melodies and their solid first-impression punch. Even if his lyrics are a little less muscular, a confetti of fears, hopes and fantasies of fatherhood, superbeings and blinding piss-elegance.

He plays one of them now, cradling his 12-string acoustic, Mark following on his own guitar, both cross-legged on the rug in the front living room. A disappointed autumn ago this was still David and Angie's bedroom; its blue walls are now a deeper shade of navy, freshly flanked by new banquette seating that looks regal but proves so uncomfortable most guests opt to slither down to the floor. On the mantelpiece, the eternal face of Garbo refuses to budge, as does Aleister Crowley's, while here, there and everywhere glisten fresh plunders from antique markets, spreading from shelf to wall to window ledge like a luxurious fungus: glassware by Lalique, Daum crystal, vases by Émile Gallé, designs by Erté and framed Edwardian fairy illustrations.

The old giant living room where northern refugees once dreamed they'd found asylum is now David and Angie's master bedroom and nursery-to-be, the walls, latterly a deep lounge green, in the process of being repainted a pale boudoir pink. The spare bedroom opposite, overlooking the garden at the rear, still has a double bed in the corner but is now David's music room, centred around a second-hand piano recently taken off a neighbour's hands for 50 quid. When he plays it the whole flat trembles like a tolling belfry and one of the keys is bust. But it's already given him 'Oh! You Pretty Things' and other as-yet-unchristened midnight tinkles.

Everything else in Flat 7, 42 Southend Road – the bathroom, the kitchen, the hall with its giant staircase to a landing to nowhere – is immovably the same. All that's really changed are beds, chairs, colours, ornaments and faces. Four months pregnant, Angie has delegated basic domestic duties to Mark's mum, born a Doris but known as 'Donna', paying her a retainer to pop across from Walnut Court and keep the cramped kitchen spick and the vast floorspace span. The indispensable Mrs Pritchett is also a welcome distraction for Peggy, David's mum, who, if she can, times her visits so she and Donna can swap mothers' troubles over a nice cup of tea.

The landlord, old Mr Hoy, still takes a keen secateur to the shrubbery front and back, and has affixed the new sign hanging from the outside porch entrance declaring the building's stately history in bold white on black: 'HADDON HALL'. Around and under the southerly side, next to the basement flat of their friends Sue and Tony Frost, is the shared garage, once the stables in the mansion's horse-drawn past, and until recently home to David's old Rover. He's since sold it in favour of something 'a little less Croydon', a black Riley RM, the sort of car a Cockney gangster might drive in an old Ealing drama. Behind it slumps another even older wooden heap of headlights and velvet upholstery vaguely recognisable as a 1930s Riley Gamecock – previous owner, at a guess, Toad of Toad Hall. It's David's hope to restore it to full highway health as soon as spare time and elbow grease allow, the measure of his efforts so far visible in the oil stains on the living-room rug where he spends rainy afternoons in greasy overalls dismantling engine parts. The very same spot where he now hunches strumming sad, baroque chords, a bit like 'Space Oddity' but tougher sounding, la-la-la-ing loose lyrics about heavy trips and space faces.

'Think you could learn it?' he asks.

Mark is younger than David, a dark head of thick shoulder-length hair like a Pepysian wig upon a face that seems older than his years. He is still 17, a schoolboy at Dulwich College where he and his mates Tim and Pete have formed their own band, Rungk: it means 'wank' in Swedish, but then schoolboys will be schoolboys, as the editors of *Oz* magazine well know, even if their circling crown prosecutors don't. David first met Mark about 18 months ago at the local Beckenham Arts Lab held in the back of the Three Tuns pub. Only after chatting about poetry, music, books and bands did they realise they were Southend Road neighbours. Soon after, David started knocking on Mark's door to borrow records or one of his electric guitars; after one visit to Walnut Court, Mark's Revox reel-to-reel tape machine crossed the road to Haddon Hall and never came back.

'And then there's this other one,' says David.

This other one is a bit faster, a bit livelier, with another scrap of a la-la lyric called 'Hang On To Yourself'. Mark catches and copies its Eddie Cochran tremble in an instant.

'Think you could teach these to the others?' says David.

By 'others' he means Mark's band, Rungk, and by 'teach' Mark realises that in David's typical two-thought-processes-ahead conversational jive, like a cinematic jump cut missing all explanatory dialogue, he is asking, no, *telling* Mark that Rungk are to be his new backing group. This, David has decided, is a done deal. Mark doesn't object. Nor, he suspects, will the rest of Rungk.

'I want to record them,' explains David. 'But not as me. You'll be the band, but it won't be called Rungk either. It'll be . . . well, I've got this . . . idea.'

David doesn't elaborate much further. One step at a time. Teach Mark the new songs, marshal his band to rehearse them, then wait until they're ready before letting them in on who their singer is. The funniest bit being even the singer doesn't know he's the singer yet. But he will. Soon as the neon Sombrero lights up again.

THREE

LAURENCE MYERS BRUSHES A SMILE through his moustache, eyes and medallion twinkling at the new silver disc mounted on his office wall. It's been over a year since he swapped accountancy for Tin Pan Alley, setting up Gem Music, his production and management stable perched above the Regent Street corner of Oxford Circus. Laurence's latest trophy, marking a quarter of a million sales for Johnny Johnson & His Bandwagon's 'Blame It On The Pony Express', is welcome reassurance it wasn't such a bad career move after all. Weeks in, and 1971 is already proving to be a very good year, thinks Laurence. Now if only he can come good on his plan to break the Tremeloes in America, and maybe have a word with God about fixing it so Arsenal win the Double, he can die a happy man, he chuckles, leaning back in his seat, admiring his silverware.

Just along the corridor is the office of the man without whom there'd be no disc on Laurence's wall. 'Pony Express' writer and Gem's golden boy Tony Macaulay, today busy relighting his Edison Lighthouse: the group who were never a real group, just four poor schmucks pretending to be the faceless session band who recorded 'Love Grows (Where My Rosemary Goes)' for the sake of the number 1 spot on *Top of the Pops*. Despite having never made the record, for the last year the fake Edison Lighthouse have been touring as *the* Edison Lighthouse. Only now, Macaulay, who still owns the group name, is launching a brand-new

Edison Lighthouse. 'The trouble with the old Edison Lighthouse,' argue the new line-up, 'was that the record ended up bigger than the group.' Which at least in the case of their own 'It's Up To You Petula' isn't something the new Edison Lighthouse ever need worry about.

'We don't bear the new Edison Lighthouse any animosity,' lie the old Edison Lighthouse, even as they're forced to shorten their name to simply 'Edison' for their rival riposte single, 'Everybody Knows'. The press ads make no bones: *'Everybody Knows is an exciting new single from the Edison everybody knows.'* Everybody knows but – old or new, Edison or Lighthouse, original fake or fake original – nobody cares.

Nobody cares about Paul Raven much either. A door along from Macaulay, the office boy of songwriter and producer Mike Leander is still hoping for his big musical break. It didn't happen with his recent cover of Sly Stone's 'Stand', though Paul still fancies himself as something of a white soul singer. Possibly it's the name that's the problem – 'Paul Raven' – not even his own but a riff on his birth name, Paul Gadd. Maybe he needs to jazz it up? Something better, starrier, with a bit more glitter, perhaps? He still waits in hope that someday soon Leander will give him something original to holler; in the meantime he's running errands, making the tea, reading *Melody Maker*, and flirting with Anya down the corridor.

Everybody flirts with Anya Wilson. Understandable, since she's no-nonsense bright, Grimsby funny, looks a bit like Brigitte Bardot, and is known from Fleet Street to White City as the hardest-working publicity girl in pop. Sadly for everybody, she also has a new boyfriend, a strapping young freelance journalist and PR from Wales called Dai. Anya works for herself, but since she does a lot for Gem, Laurence has given her a small office where she currently sits with a phone receiver clamped between shoulder and chin, tongue running over her teeth picking up the fresh taste of creamed cauliflower. An hour ago, she was in Cranks, the vegetarian restaurant a few streets away that boasts 'the best bread in town', sharing soup, herby rissoles and buckwheat noodle casserole as part of a celebration lunch with her friend, and client, Marc Bolan, and his wife June. Their treat for all her unpaid help promoting 'Ride A White Swan' by T. Rex to number 2 in the charts. So is the new fur-trimmed suede coat hanging over the back of her chair. June's just told her she wants Anya to work on all of Marc's records from now on – next time they'll pay her in more than clothes and rissoles.

It's just a pity Anya can't work the same magic on every record she's given. But then not every disc is a 'White Swan'. Sometimes, a dead duck. She squints down at the press clippings quacking dismally on her desk.

'A rather strange little piece.'

'This song has such a strange underlying feel of half doom/half madness.'

'He's so far into his own trip that this may well be a long way off commercial success.'

'Totally uncommercial and unlikely to be played.'

Rather strange, half mad, a long way off commercial success and unlikely to be played. That's the new David Bowie single in a stillborn eggshell. Even David struggles to find a good word to say about 'Holy Holy'. 'It didn't come off very well,' he apologises to Radio Luxembourg's Kid Jensen, explaining how he was trying to write a song that sounded like 'the end of the current civilisation'. Instead, he's written a song that sounds like the end of his current career. Anya punts it in vain. Or very nearly. A midweek appearance on a local current affairs programme in the Granada TV region is the best she can offer. David drives up to Manchester, and back the same day, with Anya and her boyfriend Dai for company. He sings 'Holy Holy' for the studio cameras wearing the same Mr Fish dress he last wore to the Sombrero. Civilisation doesn't end, although without David's help the cheerless streets of 1971 Manchester supply a premonition of sorts: George Best has just been suspended from United for missing training and the city wears its despair like an exploded bomb.

But Anya hasn't given up. She adores David as much as she does Marc. Sooner or later, surely, the listening public will too? Brushing the cuttings aside, sucking on her pen, she dials another number.

'Ted? Hi, it's Anya. Listen, I wanted to see if you've had any more thoughts about the new David Bowie record? Yes. For *Savile's Travels*?'

PHONE CALLS, LUNCHES, DRINKS, MEETINGS. The business of pop music is no different from espionage. MI5 or EMI, it all boils down to the same power game. Deals, favours, secrets, pressure, coercion, back-stabbings, defection, theft, embezzlement, success rewarded, failure punished, money lost, foreign travel, expensive cars, houses in the country, stories planted, rumours denied, lives ruined, fortunes made. And all the action – the *real* action, that is – takes place in the same plain buildings passers-by never look up at, staffed by women surrounded by typewriters, manila folders, filing cabinets and photocopiers, in boardrooms with closed blinds and polished tables, in offices with swivel chairs, potted plants and ashtrays. Offices like the one at the end of the corridor, along from Laurence, along from Macaulay, along from Leander and his teaboy Paul, along from Anya, along from the meeting room where they held the Christmas drinks party where Paul and Anya danced the twist. The office of Tony Defries.

Defries does not look like your typical spymaster. That's what makes him a good one. He's a legal eagle in raver's clothing, his wardrobe groovy casual in keeping with his bushy afro hair. To see him from afar you'd imagine he smells of dope and calls everyone 'baby': up close, he smells of fat cigars and is hypnotically courteous in his every dealing. It's all chess to Defries. See, the punter – the man and woman in the street, the screaming girl in Row C, the spotty boy among the Woolies' record racks – they think it's all about *the bands* and *the singers* and *the songs*. Let them believe it. The fairy story that says records get to number 1 simply because they, the people, *like* them. Don't blow the whistle. Don't tell them that Clive Dunn isn't number 1 just now with 'Grandad' *just* because he's in *Dad's Army*. Don't let them know he got there because somebody, somewhere, broke balls and bar bills to get it played on Tony Blackburn and to book Dunn on *Stewpot*, and made sure the poor sods at the pressing plants worked extra shifts and pulled all the other levers that people like Defries, unseen behind the curtain, pull to outfox the competition. *This* is the real business of pop music. Defries's business. Putting the frighteners on flash little twerps.

It's like his current problem. The one on his desk, same as the one on Anya's desk. *'Totally uncommercial and unlikely to be played.'* Not what Defries was expecting when he first came to Laurence last summer, asking to join Gem in return for bringing them the management reins of his fresh scalp, David Bowie. He takes a pensive puff on his cigar. The bad tidings vanish in a cloud of smoke, just for a second, before thinning again like a harbour fog rolling back from a shipwreck. '*Unlikely.*' Hmm. Still, not '*impossible*'. Anya swears to him she's trying everything she can. Maybe. So, what to *do* with the boy?

The answer is typed out on a sheet of paper he pulls from the loose pile beside him. An itinerary from Mercury Records, Chicago, for a round trip to the USA by their English client, David Bowie, for the purposes of promoting his album *The Man Who Sold The World*, exclusively released there a couple of months ago, for a period of approximately four weeks. No performances. Just 'rapping' to the press and radio, city to city, coast to coast. The budget is minimal. They'll only pay for David's flight, and where possible he'll be staying and travelling with Mercury employees and industry acquaintances to save on travel and hotel bills. Meaning, while he's there, it'll be up to David and David alone to sell himself.

Defries takes another puff, gazing out through the blinds. Grey–white skies over London as 5,000 tills ring daily for The Mixtures' 'Pushbike Song'. Hmm. It's all a bit of a godsend, really. Britain just isn't happening for David right now. Best thing for him, stick him on a plane to America, see what damage he can do out there. He's nothing to lose by trying, nothing to gain by staying here smelling the slow rot of 'Holy Holy'. Do everybody a bit of good, get him out of the country for a while, out of sight, out of trouble. Out of Defries's hair so he can concentrate on his next queen's gambit.

Cigar tip smouldering, he turns to that week's dispatches from the front lines. *Melody Maker, Record Mirror, Disc and Music Echo, Sounds* and the *New Musical Express*. Seems Marc Bolan's using his tradecraft well. Much intelligence on George Harrison's 'My Sweet Lord' and Elton John's 'Your Song'. Neil Young is *'the superstar of the Seventies'*. Possible disinformation? We'll see. And Stevie Wonder's in town. Hmm. Now then, that's *very* interesting . . .

ANGIE HELPS HIM PACK. She doesn't want him to leave, but she also wants him to go. He needs to, for all their sakes: his, hers and the 21-week-old starchild kicking inside her. Their last night together before his flight it is David who worries and Angie who reassures him. She will be fine. *They* will be fine. She has her friend, Sue, from the basement flat downstairs, and Donna and Mark over the road, and even Peggy a few streets away. She will not be alone, she whitely lies, knowing that there will be sleepless nights of kicks and cramps in an empty bed, wondering who's sharing his an Atlantic Ocean away, pretending none of it hurts. No, David *must* go. Even the cover of this month's *Vogue* tells him so.

'JOURNEY TO THE USA.'

So does the television, hissing with Cold War panic in the late Friday film, *Invasion of the Body Snatchers*. Strange mannequin-spewing seedpods from outer space and people pretending to be who they are not.

His paperwork and passport lie folded and ready with his boots, his blue fur coat, his cigarettes and a case containing clothes, notepads, a toilet bag and two dresses by Mr Fish, all stacked together in the corner like an unpainted still life titled *Leaving Tomorrow*.

Today becomes tomorrow at midnight. Their last hours of touch and warmth and taste and smell before each vanish into a ghost dimension of memory and negative space and disembodied voices down a telephone earpiece. On screen, the alien seedpods are spilling over the interstate.

'THEY'RE ALREADY HERE!'

In what last dreams his body snatches on his Beckenham pillow, David is already journeying to the USA.

FOUR

JET ENGINES BANSHEE-SCREECH. Ears pop, knees fizz and gravity tips from spine to toes. Windows smaller than TV screens whip away tarmac, mown grass and chain-link fences to a waltzer ride of white and blue. Disbelief suspended, prayers gasped, fragile mortality is now an eight-hour hostage to the unsentimental laws of aerodynamic drag and thrust.

The plane gently tilts as clouds raise a curtain on a railway model of building-block houses, baize fields and dinky cars. Little England, falling ten thousand, eleven thousand, twelve thousand feet.

Look at it, way down there. Already insignificant isle of postal strikes, hot pants fever and the last days of the threepenny bit. Braindead with bobbybeat fictions of *Dixon of Dock Green* as black bones break against holding cell doors. The Angry Brigade plotting anarchy with homemade bombs, and barracks of boy soldiers shining their boots ready for slaughter in Belfast.

Thirteen, fourteen, fifteen thousand feet. Down there, Susan George sets her bottom lip to pout on the Cornish set of *Straw Dogs*. Guy the Gorilla stares at the dumb animals on the other side of his cage in London Zoo. Sid James listens to Sammy Davis Jr on his Daimler's new eight-track cartridge player. Clive Dunn mildews at number 1. Banana split children cry wally-ball havoc, and schoolgirls moan in darkened bedrooms for Marc Bolan.

Sixteen, seventeen, eighteen thousand feet. Down there, a neon Sombrero awaits evening ignition. Nods itch to follow winks in the cruising Mayfair shadows of Half Moon Street. A skinhead proudly tells a magazine he'd 'rather bash a queer than a paki' because 'I can't bear the idea of a geezer wot's bent'. Acidheads turn blue trying to trip on Parkinson's drugs, and Jagger's arse humps on a 43-foot West End screen.

Nineteen, twenty, twenty-one thousand feet. Down there, where a 4 oz jar of Nescafe still costs five shillings. Another busty Scandinavian from the cast of *Lust for a Vampire* follows her co-stars to become the latest *Golden Shot* 'Maid of the Month'. Biba girls follow the glossies' spring trend for *'romantic Garbo fashions tarted up in the '71 style'*. Doctor Who struggles in his first TV battle with The Master, and no radio station plays 'Holy Holy'.

Twenty-two, twenty-three, twenty-four thousand feet. Down there, sweet mama Angie and papa's little kicker. His dead father's ashes feeding worms in the soil of a crematorium rose bed. His half-brother Terry, dosed up in Cane Hill mental hospital, and their mum, Peggy, making sandwiches for her next visit there.

Twenty-five thousand feet and climbing. David, alone, up here. Out of sight of down there. Slipping through a crack in the sky. Lost in space. Into the unknown.

AMERICA WELCOMES HIM with folded arms. Timedrunk, he steps off the plane into a cold white world of tannoy voices and impatient feet. He is here, the here of Elvis Presley and Batman, of every Hollywood film he's ever seen in every Saturday morning ABC, yet in the immediate hereness of being here it's as if there's a filter missing. America doesn't flicker at 24 frames a second in vivid VistaVision. America feels temporally normal. Change clothes and accents and this could be Croydon. It's only his heart that tells him. *America*. Little Richard, Charles Mingus, Andy Warhol. The herds plod on to Border Security, David following in a disbelieving haze, waiting for the movie to start.

Here is Virginia, the Old Dominion, Washington Dulles International Airport, over 3,500 miles from the Fulham Road where David first took from its boutique hanger the fake fur coat the colour of van Gogh blue now resting on his shoulders. A blue all the bluer for the golden hair above it and the pink trousers below, shimmering its way to the front of the queue like a giant Liquorice Allsort. Suspicious epaulettes beckon him to the immigration desk where he smiles as freaky a smile as ever begged for entry and slides forward his passport with a chinking bangled wrist. It is picked up by hands made of meatloaf, *Perry Mason*, the World Series, *Gunsmoke*, apple sauce, Johnny Cash, bar pretzels, Miller High Life, station wagons, *Playboy* centrefolds, hosed lawns, Twinkies and President Nixon. Watchtower eyes flick from page to person.

Name: David Robert Jones.

Hmm.

Profession: Entertainer.

Hmm.

Height: 5 ft, 10 in.

Five-twelve in those heels.

Eyes: Blue

Which one?

Special peculiarities: Enlarged pupil left eye.

Woah!

A rectangular black-and-white photograph taken 18 months ago shows a serious young man with short Harpo Marx curls. This looks more like a David, more like a Mr Jones. The creature on the other side of the desk looks like a cross between Myra Breckinridge and Alice the Goon. The gatekeeper presses his tongue against the side of his mouth, sucking in a loud breath, a free hand softly pinching the end of his chin.

'It says you're an "entertainer", Mr Jones?'

'Yes. I sing.'

A silent second passes in an hour.

'What's the purpose of your visit to the United States?'

'I'm here to do promotion. My record.'

And another one.

'You have a work visa?'

'No, I'm . . . I'm not performing.'

A pin begs to drop.

'So why are you here?'

'Talking. Interviews. Press, radio, that sort of thing. The . . . the record company invited me. They've paid for me to come.'

Blinkless hammerhead shark eyes stare.

'What's the company?'

'Mercury Records.'

Not good enough.

'You have an address?'

'I've got a phone number. There's someone coming here to meet me.'

Unblinking orbs swivel in gun turrets from document to David and back again. Until dill pickle fingers reach for a walkie-talkie.

'Mr Jones, I'm going to have to ask you to step aside . . .'

SO, THIS IS AMERICA. After 45 minutes, United States Customs and Border Protection run out of reasons not to believe David is who he says he is, kicking him through to arrivals with a stamped passport and a rifled suitcase. The man from Mercury Records is there to meet him and under his direction the movie finally starts. A slow decompression, nothing too sharp and shocking: gently over the East Coast, Maryland, Baltimore, Philadelphia, highway signs, diners, coffee, hamburgers, and denimed disc jockeys asking, like, how come he was born David Jones but calls himself David Bowie? He tells them he took it from the Texas town, and the adventurer, Jim.

'It's Scottish as well, and there's a knife involved. It just sounded good.'

He's asked about Elton John, who he doesn't know, and Marc Bolan, who he does, and whether his surname is pronounced 'Bau-ee' or 'Boo-ee' or 'Bow-ee'. And then it hits him with the suddenness of being woken from a sleepwalk. The beautiful realisation that nobody here, not one person, has the faintest glimmer of an inkling of a scrap of a crumb of a clue who he is. Nobody knows him as the cute curly-haired boy singing about Major Tom because nobody's heard 'Space Oddity'. Nobody's pinned David's face on their wall because it hasn't been in any magazines. Nobody thinks of him as a one-hit wonder because he's still on square zero. He is unknown, a new face with no history, whoever he wants to tell them he is. An LP artist. A shaven-headed transvestite. A jazz musician. An escaped prisoner. If he wanted, he could even pass off as a juggler named Johnny Dean. *'Avin' a laugh, you see, with my image.*

And they'd drink it all as gospel.

NEW YORK CITY. City of night, even in the never-slept mid-morning hustle as David beetles his first steps over steaming gum-trodden sidewalks that wind between the tower blocks like gaps in old floorboards. Squashed down by a manmade sky of black glass and white concrete and the physical gut tug of the Earth's wobbly spin as choirs of girders creak slander to gravity. An urgent, inexorable orchestra of humans, architecture, automobiles and electricity, each trying to smash the last cymbal of a crescendo that never ends. Noon or midnight, it's all the same volume, all the same speed. Watch hands rat-a-tat like Gene Krupa's drumsticks and every greedy hour shoots dice to steal more minutes. New York is being locked in a car with no brakes that never quite crashes. Cling on and scream. Or enjoy the ride.

David's begins on West 57th Street. Midtown Holiday Inn. Plain walls, a bed, a bathroom, a telephone and a remote-control television set. Click on. NBC News, an old *Bewitched*, a daytime soap, kids screaming about spaghetti sauce. Click off. Just another man in a box suspended in Manhattan space, but already he hears the city whisper its filthy secrets. Along the street, three blocks east, the studio where Charles Mingus made *Oh Yeah*, all those wham-bam notes David first heard from Terry that still zigzag off his ceiling in Haddon Hall. Only a few blocks south, where The Velvet Underground recorded 'I'm Waiting For The Man'. A little further north by northeast, five blocks, maybe six, the restaurant where Stanley Kubrick first met Arthur C. Clarke to discuss turning one of his short stories into *2001: A Space Odyssey*; and if he hadn't, and if it wasn't, then David would never have written 'Space Oddity'. Brixton-born and Bromley-bred, David is New York-wired. Now, for the first time, aged 24, he plugs himself into the mains.

Green light stampedes, horns beeping meaningless Morse code, north to Central Park, barebranched and greylaked, boots crushing jagged yellow leaves that look cut by scissors, past bronze poets and mad hatters and faceless old men peeking over scarves sitting alone on benches so long and wide they look twice as lonely until, there like a sacred temple among the trees, the Metropolitan Museum of Art. David fumbles in his coat pocket for the discretionary dollar entry fee and follows the signs up the marble stairs to the painting galleries. Florentine, Venetian, Renaissance, Baroque; foreboding El Greco clouds to biblical Tintoretto and soft sfumato Madonnas. Punched by Picasso, kicked by de Kooning and walloped by Pollock, his eyes sting with so much glory. And crave yet more.

Times Square, head smashed by Coca-Cola neon, Kent cigarettes, Yashica cameras, Bulova watches, Canadian Club, Castro convertibles, Beefeater gin, hoardings big enough to read from space yelling *Hair*, *Applause* and *Love Story*. The city perfume of carbon monoxide, tobacco, fried onions, cologne, gum and sweat. Cocktail bars, spaghetti houses, drugstores, newsstands, hot dogs, showgirls without stages, cowboys without horses, ugly buyers and beautiful sellers, cops and bums and piss-stained lunatics yakking about 'Jesus' making atheists of anyone close enough to smell them. Where David, in his blue fur coat, pink trousers and boots, hair whipping like Gilda in the crosswinds, heads eastwards in the shadow of the Hotel Claridge, where Joe Buck tossed his torn postcard home from a ninth-floor window in *Midnight Cowboy*. A woman suddenly stops him. She just *has* to ask, ever so American, which species of animal is his jacket made of?

David answers, ever so English. 'Teddy bear.'

She laughs a rattling laugh like ice at the bottom of a shot glass. The kind you only ever hear in New York City. David commits it to the echo of memory and waltzes on. Led by his appetites, to bookstores, record shops and tobacconists, the 'world famous' Nat Sherman's by the Public Library, a city within a city of wooden drawers, cigar boxes and the intoxicating aroma of cherry, leather and firewood sweetening his every breath. David buys a pack of Sherman's custom-made Cigaretellos: thin and brown, somewhere between a cigarette and a cigarillo. 'Queen size' for men – and women.

It is only late afternoon, but David has a schedule to keep with more men from Mercury Records and their local pick of intense rock critics who, after listening to his latest album, have decided he's the product of *'violence, bloodshed, war, the technological curse, lacerations of the mind, tears which can't be kept from falling, the terrible loneliness of space, the dark abyss of murderer's eyes, foreboding cellars and the madness which creeps softly and inexorably towards the foot of the bed'.* And that's one of his sympathetic reviews.

He meets them back at the Holiday Inn where they sit on the end of his bed and ask him if he writes to gain or lose his identity?

'Possibly to understand it,' he says. 'I don't think either to lose or gain.'

Outside, the wind has turned wrathful. Scaffolding snaps like cocktail sticks and in a timpani of shattering glass and clanging steel the roads below become a traffic no-go. Upper storeys sway seasick and the subways flood with twitchy drones sent home early by reluctant bosses. The Mercury party dodge the storm debris to a West Side trattoria where David lines his stomach, then to Greenwich Village to line his head in the basement crypt of the Gaslight Café, its rafters still waiting for another young Dylan to re-pin it to history. David's first proper night in the city of night is spent envying the beauty of 'Misty Roses', 'The Lady Came From Baltimore', 'Reason To Believe' and other songs that fall from Tim Hardin's lips as sad and dreamy as the heroin shrivelling his veins. When the show is over, David tries to pay Hardin a visit backstage: neither to lose nor gain but possibly to understand. But the tiny dressing room is already too full and David another milling nobody on the wrong side of the door.

Back on street level, the corner of Bleecker and MacDougal, where David stands twilight-stoned like an album cover lost in the moment of a missing camera. The sky above is starless. Midtown, neon mosquitoes draw all the blood there is to suck as sirens yawn like the living dead. Crepuscular cabs slither lane to lane; in one a 33-year-old nightshifter the garage know as 'Phil' rides the avenues like they're lines on staff paper, every block the same note repeating one after the other, every green light a new bar, every robbery-risking fare a means to an end between his next concert tour of strange metropolis mood music.

And as Philip Glass keeps cruising Uptown, as David drifts into wakeless sleep under Holiday Inn sheets, in her East Side fifth-floor apartment a 65-year-old woman sits alone in the corner window overlooking the white necklace of lights on the Queensboro bridge. On one shelf, a hardback volume of *As I Lay Dying*, on another, the down-hearted blues of Bessie Smith yells silently from unspinning LP grooves. The world at a safe distance, as she desires it, she lights a thin, brown queen-size filter-tip – her favourite brand, Nat Sherman's Cigaretellos – and blows smoke at the imprisoned reflection of Greta Garbo.

FIVE

ALL IS LONELINESS. The guilty dawn of turned-out lights, cold griddles, pulled shutters, locked doors and the loose change of yesterday's lies. The same daily withdrawal before the next fix of nightfall.

East River boats belch a rude good morning. She steps out to greet it in a dark fur coat over a dun cotton shirt and trouser suit, colours carefully chosen to vanish against Manhattan's concrete frieze. Her hair is tied back, a scarf knotted around her neck, her face obscured by thick-rimmed sunglasses. But still, they recognise her. The desperate ones wait at the end of her street like bad detectives, stunned by her brisk pace as they puff ten paces behind. She pauses to peer in shop windows, her rear-view mirrors to identify clumsy foes, plotting how best to shake them off, whether the next corner, the next set of lights or, if needs must, a sudden jaywalk. Up First, west on 57th, down Madison, cut over to Fifth at 51st, down 49th and back again. She trusts no one and risks nothing. It's enough that a handful of stores have reached a patient telepathic understanding: no eye contact, no small talk, just 'please' and 'thank you' and sell her whatever groceries she asks for without so much as a smile or a wink or a blush betraying they know she's *Mata Hari*, *Queen Christina* and *Camille* of a million ticket stubs. It's the very reason she came to settle in the city of night. To be alone.

Garbo slips back home through the same Midtown streets where David, refreshed, also slips, never seeing her, or if he does, never recognising her as the goddess on his mantelpiece 3,000 miles away. His is a different trail of solitude, leading him down Sixth Avenue to the corner of 54th near the Warwick Hotel, where a homeless man with straggly white hair stands wrapped in an army blanket over robes like Moses, holding a large spear and wearing a Viking helmet.

Moondog. David heard about him last night, how most days you'll find him here, always on the same corner selling his sad spooky poems or playing his sad spooky tunes on the sad spooky instruments he fashioned himself that all sound like crying Japanese peasants. Sometimes he howls words – *'all is loneliness'* – in such a voice as neither Garbo nor God would beg to differ.

David approaches Moondog and in his polite English manner asks if he can buy him some lunch. Moondog accepts but doesn't budge from his spot. Taking his cue, a few minutes later David returns with takeout coffee and sandwiches. They sit down side by side on concrete steps above the sidewalk, the robed Viking and the long-haired boy in the blue fur coat. This being New York City, nobody looks twice. David asks Moondog how he came to be Moondog. He tells him his real name is Louis, he was born in Kansas and raised in Wyoming and Missouri. He is 54 years old. Even though he's American, Moondog likes to think of himself as 'a European living in exile'. David nods affinity but Moondog stares through him with dark pitted eyes that haven't once opened. It's then he realises. Moondog is blind.

'I'm considered to be in the present, even avant-garde,' continues Moondog, 'whereas melodically and harmonically I'm very much in the past. But the present becomes the past just as the future becomes the present.'

He tells David about his instruments, one called an 'oo', another called a 'trimba'. Being blind he composes by Braille. Besides the incalculable sadness of human existence, Moondog likes to write about the solar system, witches, Charlie Parker and Thor. He had an album out on Columbia about a year ago. 'It didn't sell.' David asks what it's called. '*Moondog*,' says Moondog, draining his Styrofoam cup. 'But I'll make another,' he adds, hauling himself back up with a firm hold of his spear. 'It's like I say. Today is yesterday's tomorrow, which is now. Thanks for the coffee.'

David leaves the man born Louis, now Moondog, where he found him. Where he'll still be tomorrow, in the now of then before the present becomes the past in the infinite loneliness of the city of night.

'**SEE THE VELVET UNDERGROUND AT THE ELECTRIC CIRCUS.**' David spies the ad and his eyes turn crystal. It bears the same cartoon subway entrance featured on the cover of their new album, *Loaded*, which David heard for the first time only yesterday when his new journalist friend Ed played it to him. He'd have fallen in love with it just the same had he first heard it at home in Beckenham. The fact that he first hears it *here*, as all around him the steam from the A trains hiss 'Sweet Jane' and a million fire escapes clang 'Rock & Roll', to load up on *Loaded* in its New York womb, is like a French kiss from God. To actually *see* the group live – a heavenly ascension.

The Electric Circus turns out to be an old dancehall down the East Village on St Mark's Place, a popular live venue and discotheque until nine months ago when someone, possibly Hells Angels, set off a bomb during a Sly Stone gig. Nobody was killed, and nobody charged, but the Electric Circus hasn't been the same since. David knows none of this and wouldn't care if he did: so long as The Velvet Underground were playing, he'd foxtrot round a minefield.

In a dip of lights and scattering of whoops they suddenly appear. Apart from their tomboyish drummer, Moe, The Velvet Underground look like any other rock band: shaggy hair, jeans, Chelsea boots. David fixes unblinking idol eyes on their curly-haired singer, Lou Reed. He doesn't move much, just stands there, picking and singing. But it's the songs he sings. David's favourites 'I'm Waiting For The Man', 'White Light/White Heat', and the new ones, 'Sweet Jane' and 'Rock & Roll'. Lowlife tales of high romance, street-level beat sonnets of sex and drugs, like if Kerouac had been into R&B instead of bebop and had Sal Paradise speaking in tongues over 'Long Tall Sally'. Maybe the greatest rock'n'roll songs David's ever heard.

Tonight cannot be a repeat of Tim Hardin. He *must* make it backstage and speak to Lou Reed by any means necessary. An English accent proves enough. A visitor – a *fan* – 'from London', and the dressing-room door opens.

David, say hello to The Velvet Underground.

He's beside Lou in a blink. So much that he wants to say, so much he wants to know. He starts by telling Lou he must be their biggest fan in England, and that he's a singer too, and he does his own version of 'I'm Waiting For The Man', and it's just a crime that they're not known over there . . .

'Uh-huh.'

. . . and *Loaded*, well, that just knocked him out, especially 'Sweet Jane', and could Lou tell him the chords . . .

'Hmm.' Lou scratches his head.

. . . and he's not just saying it but, honestly, Lou, you're just the most fantastic songwriter . . .

'Eh . . .' Lou shifts uncomfortably. 'Look, buddy. I'm not Lou Reed . . .'

. . . Uh?

Ladies and gentlemen! In tonight's episode of The Velvet Underground Live At The Electric Circus, *the part of Lou Reed, who sadly couldn't be here on account of the fact that he quit the group five months ago, was played by Mr Doug Yule – latterly their bass player, now by default their frontman, who can be heard sharing lead vocals on their latest album,* Loaded *– out now in all good record stores! Also appearing were original group members Sterling Morrison, on guitar, and Moe Tucker, drums, and introducing Mr Walter Powers on bass guitar. The part of the naïve English fan who makes a jackass of himself backstage was played by our special guest star, Mr David Bowie.*

This has been a mistaken-identity production.

THREE AND A HALF THOUSAND MILES AWAY, a telephone rings. Connecting Beckenham, England, 658 1577. Angie picks up.

'DAVID!'

And the windowpanes shiver.

He is standing in a phone box on 46th and Broadway, staring through greasy glass as fast lights and slow shadows twist against a concrete canvas in the dying light of afternoon. A world which pops like a balloon when he hears her voice, familiar and disembodied, intimate yet abstract. Coins drop quick and tender words rush quicker. Yes, he misses her. Yes, she and the baby are fine. No, she won't try to finish painting the bedroom ceiling in case she has an accident. No, he hasn't worn either of his Mr Fish dresses yet. Last coins fumble and clang.

'Oh, and David . . .' A sudden crackle of nerves. 'Guess what? Terry's here.'

He is silent. Lost cents dwindle.

'*Terry?*'

'Yes. He's staying here.'

'You mean he's run away?'

'Yes.'

'Is he there with you now?'

'Yes.'

'Can you speak?'

'No.'

'You sure everything's OK?'

'Yes.'

Beep!

'I love you.'

Beep beep!

'I lo—'

Beep beep beep!

The cold, dead mechanical purr.

In Beckenham, Angie replaces the receiver. Outside it is a cloudless blue English noon. Terry stands, gazing out into the garden, drawing on his cigarette. Its tip glows, briefly, like a light in the skyline of a city he will never see.

OH, TERRY. If you could only see what David sees with his eyes. From New York to Michigan, Wisconsin, Illinois, Texas and California. Freeways, skyscrapers, El trains, TV show cop cars, Piggly Wigglys, water towers, trash cans, basketball hoops, miniskirts, sideburns, afros and brown paper grocery bags. Channel-hopping Lucille Ball, *The Partridge Family* and *Alias Smith and Jones* – 'the most wanted men in the West – new for Thursday nights on ABC!' Clawing Holiday Inn sheets with Beatle-dazed hippie chicks too easily turned on by his fish'n'chips accent. Label offices, record stores and radio stations, picking up more sonic shrapnel of weird than he can fit in his suitcase. Bebopping Chicago and sucking on Ginsberg's bones in the cheap Chinese basement of San Francisco's Woey Loy Goey. More disc jockeys introducing 'David Booee' and more serious men from serious rock papers asking him serious questions about revolution and religion. Giving strange answers about Buddhism and the Third Reich that linger in scribbled lyrics about sinking in quicksand. Telling them all about *you*, Terry. Your song, 'All The Madmen'.

'Based on my brother,' says David. 'The majority of the people in my family have been in some kind of mental institution. My brother would be happy to spend the rest of his life there – mainly because most of the people are on the same wavelength as him. And he's not a freak, he's a very straight person.'

Unlike David, brazenly breaking out his Mr Fish dress at last for Nixon's silent majority to see.

The Deep South swings to 'Rose Garden' and here he comes – *I beg your pardon!* – like a pink Nancy thorn in its side reminding 'em that life ain't all pork'n'beans but a never-ending Alamo to be fought against *goddamn commies*, *atheists*, *fairies*, *dykes*, *kikes*, *niggers*, *spicks* and anyone else who don't want their sons to be another of Uncle Sam's baby killers, rapists, junkies, cripples and barely identifiable body-bag slop.

But Houston, Texas, isn't ready for this particular English rose. David sees the barrel of the gun before the face behind the trigger. A face like a saddle, tanned and leathery, eyes of bourbon and women's broken bones, lips noisily smacking a plug of tobacco. The sort of face that shoots as easily as it chews.

'If it weren't agin the law' – *smack!* – 'I'd blow yer brains out.'

David, in his blue dress, turns a cloudy white.

'Quit town' – *schlup!* – 'you goddam fag!'

It's like Chas says in *Performance*. 'America. It's a blinding place.'

AS TEXAS CLENCHES tight its lone star ass, in England a queerer sort of spring is in blossom. Loves that dared not speak their name now yell them bold as fishmongers.

'I suppose I'm a communist homosexual junkie.'

Lionel Bart – the virtually bankrupt 40-year-old Cockney composer of Cliff's 'Living Doll', the musical *Oliver!*, casual acquaintance of David Bowie and the latest managerial acquisition by Laurence Myers of Gem Music – comes out of his closet on page 11 of the *Daily Mirror*. Others still rummage coyly in the coat hangers. Robin Stewart, the 24-year-old who plays Sid James's teenage son in new sitcom *Bless This House*, chooses the cover of *TV Times* to announce that he and his wife Jill share the same wardrobe: hip-hugging brocade trousers, a voile of buttercup yellow, a splash of jasmine oil. What's hers is his. Androgyny, he admits, can be a brutal business. 'I was accosted not so long ago at Charing Cross station by a little Scottish chap who said, "Are you queer or something? Are you an old queen? Are you gay?" And when I invited him to call a policeman he spat in my face and walked off.' But Robin, who also drinks beer and smokes a pipe, swears he's never upset when mistaken for a homosexual. 'It doesn't worry me what people think – I am what I am.'

The lesbians who frequent London's Gateways club are what they are, which is all very well so long as nobody else knows they exist. When a TV documentary crew lifts the lid one Tuesday after *News at Ten*, all Sapphic hell breaks loose. The Gateways isn't shown, only the lives of the patrons. Just good-looking girls into other good-looking girls, laughing, loving and smooching to the Bee Gees. *Where would I be without my woman?* The day after broadcast one of them is sacked from her job and evicted from her flat by a boss and a landlord who remember her face but not the programme's title: *The Important Thing Is Love*. But watching in suburban prisons after their parents have gone to bed are enough young girls already too long at life's razor's edge who will wake up tomorrow in a world less lonely. Sweet be their under-the-blanket transistor dreams. Sing, Frankie Valli. '*You're ready now.*'

For some the queer spring blooms too slow. For whom women explaining why lesbian sex is better than heterosexual sex on national television is not enough. Who think the best way to open up the floodgates is to close down the Gateways. Marching through its green door and telling the patrons that by hiding themselves away they're acting like oppressed victims isn't the worst of the Gay Liberation Front's ideas. Unplugging the jukebox is. Call a dyke what you like but don't stop the music unless you fancy being dragged out hair-first by a pitprop of a barmaid named Smithy. 'GAY IS GOOD!' chant a hundred other well-meaning brothers and sisters waiting outside on the corner of Bramerton Street. 'FUCK OFF!' roars Smithy and promptly phones the rozzers. Minutes later, 30 of them screech up and start randomly nicking anyone in sight. One girl is hit in the face and poked up the arse with a truncheon. Two innocent lads are punted in the back of the van just for standing at a nearby bus stop; neither are gay and neither have even heard of the Gay Liberation Front but tomorrow they'll both be a quid's fine poorer for 'obstructing the free passage of the highway'. They and others too slow to scarper spend a cold night sharing a Chelsea police cell, save one poor dear who spends it in solitary for daring to pucker a fruity *'Oooh!'* when frisked. The total sum of the evening's achievements amount to 13 charge sheets and a lifetime ban for anyone daft enough to return to the Gateways wearing a GLF badge. The presses of the underground hippie papers rattle with inky mirth.

'The Gay Liberation Front would seem to the casual observer to be singularly lacking in gaiety . . .'

SIX

A SHADOW PASSES GAILY over Garbo's star in the sidewalk before pausing under the pagoda façade of Grauman's Chinese Theatre. Today's feature: *The Great White Hope*. David hoorays for Hollywood.

Los Angeles, his last measure of America. City of angels and fortress of vampires. The endless backlot stretching far beyond the studio gates along flat earth miles of déjà vu avenues; in every bar and grill where every drink is served like it's another screen test; in lives that aren't lived but printed in daily rushes; in shipped-in palm trees shrugging guiltily against the matte painted sky, winding up into the hills of the headline haves with their poolside views peering down upon the have-nots like a pornographic Pompeii of mock-exotic architecture, Quaaludes and rhinoplasty, waiting for the John Wayne voice of God to yell 'CUT!'

The town's tinsel sparkles only dimly in Hamburger Hamlet where David savours the fries and onions of outrageous portions at the behest of his painfully enthusiastic gnomelike chaperone. It's another of Mercury Records' infinite supply of regional publicists, this one arriving in a satin jacket with hair like a well-whacked shuttlecock and a face which even when smiling radiates the helpless appeal of a forlorn Jewish grandma who's misplaced her purse.

His name is Rodney Bingenheimer and his local celebrity that of 'the Mayor of Sunset Strip', a nickname he prizes despite the disinterest of any other living person who might contest this office. Rodney looks a proper Rodney but being from Los Angeles has no idea what that means: that he doesn't is the tragedy of a man for whom not being born a Beatle is a terminal illness. England is his Lapland and its every new US chart invader another Father Christmas – even David, whose failure, so far, to invade any charts drains none of the glitter from Rodney's eyes: it's enough that he is British, that he sings, and that he is here. Nor does his damselish attire bother Rodney. The opposite – it confirms David's aristocracy as hallowed Carnaby Street gentry: long hair like Robert Plant, girlish clothes like Mick Jagger, and those teeth, like so much bent canteen cutlery shoved in too small a drawer. It's the teeth that seal it. David is the real bad-Brit-dentures rock'n'roll deal.

Rodney has brought him to Hamburger Hamlet because 'this is where the stars eat'. The only stars David sees are the ones twinkling in the waitresses' ears, but then Hollywood never disappoints in its speed to disappoint. There is a real city here somewhere, the city *down there*, under the smog, in the lost Angeles of Main Street hustlers, queens and fairies David reads about in the holier than holy revelations of John Rechy but never sees from the passenger seat of Rodney's Cadillac convertible – borrowed like everything else in this town, including time. Instead, he is ferried around the iron lungs of old Hollywood and all its wheezing imitations of dreams already dead and buried in rusting metal cans. Down the Strip's tourist-neon jungle, with all its statutory rapists and eager prey seeking solace in shared fears of ugliness, old age and self-worth. To the 'world famous' Whisky a Go Go, no longer the club it used to be five years ago when it didn't live up to the club it ought to be then. To Rodney's 'friend' Kim Fowley, a wired and wiry producer and singer who makes records called 'Born To Make You Cry' and whose dismembering gaze promises infinitely worse. Chasing the night up into the hills, on to highball-lipped soirées in the Manson-stalked homes of the sunstroked and starfucked who take David on Rodney's word as 'the biggest thing out of England since Elton John'.

The new Elton is urged to perform, and since this is a private gathering, as a visiting alien he can. David's stage is a waterbed where he wobbles cross-legged with a borrowed acoustic guitar. And slowly sinks. A Jacques Brel number about the whores and belching sailors of Amsterdam is followed by some of his own about lobotomies and general mental distress. Hollywood rewards in second nature with lying-eyed applause, the percussive relief that a pooped party may yet be rescued once he leaves the building.

Thanks to Rodney, he does, briskly chauffeured further up into the hills where at last he finds another stranger in town somewhere on his wavelength. That they're sat naked in a bath of milk and holding a bowling ball says as much about David as it does about the search for intelligent life in Hollywood. Her name is Ultra Violet and this is her party, though not her house, nor by choice her city. Like David, hers is a foreign body – originally French – and an artist's head: the face a sphinxy gaze framed by eyebrows like a Cocteau drawing, the hair a dark spillage of corkscrews shimmering iridescent lilac, same as her chosen name. As Isabelle she was first discovered by Dalí; as Ultra immortalised by Warhol as one of his 16mm underground 'Superstars', a society fame that led to a blink-and-missable cameo in *Midnight Cowboy* before the fatal gravitational drag to California. And so here she is, bathing like an Egyptian queen for the benefit of a few invited members of the press and attendant good time Charlies, Rodneys and Davids. When his chance comes, he can't help but ask the question everyone asks Ultra Violet. Andy Warhol: what's he really like?

'Andy's like me,' replies a voice like a cool summer's eve on the Champs-Élysées. 'We both see beyond the spectrum of light . . .'

SOFT SUNLIGHT BOUNCES through Juliet balcony windows, dazzling green in the eyes of Marc Bolan. He sits regally on a velvet Chesterfield camelback sofa, dressed in Mr Freedom rainbows and satins, his dark curls reflected through the etched castle logo of Glasgow brewers G. & J. Maclachlan in the enormous antique pub mirror on the wall behind him. In front of it, a record player and rows of stacked albums and singles, Marc's own discs face-front beside others by the Rolling Stones and Gene Vincent. A silver disc for 'Ride A White Swan' gleams victoriously atop one of the many cases and cabinets straining with the weight of so many lamps, chess sets, his superstitious Pan statue, carved hourglasses, pewter picture frames, more records wobbling in ready-totumble Pisa towers and books upon books upon books of poetry, fairy tales and the paintings of Salvador Dalí. Now a quarter-million-selling singles artist and certifiably *'a star'* as of last week's *Melody Maker*, Marc has moved up in the world and its London postcodes, home now an iron-balustraded first-floor flat in Little Venice, Maida Vale, with its blue carpets, earthy patterned Eastern rugs, deep green walls, floral curtains, purple throws and red cushions. A Technicolor dream for a Technicolor dreamer.

'I've arranged to see Fellini when he comes over, to see if I can write something for him.'

Words rushing faster than the speed of truth splinter in shorthand runes in the notepad of the journalist sitting opposite, their other hand mid-fork in the plate of spinach pie on their lap. In another corner of the living room sits its baker, Marc's wife June, waiting for the right moment to slink off into the kitchen in her patched Levi's to reappear with a Lyons chocolate cake for afters. It's their third visitor this week. The serious stinky-boy inkies, the weak-kneed girls' weeklies, the hip and the hippies, the dolly gossipers and teenyboppers, one by one they ascend the stairs of 31 Clarendon Gardens for pie, cake, honeyed toast and all the ego their readers can stomach. None leave wanting.

'The few people who are saying we've sold out – their outlook is so narrow. I'm pleased T. Rex are no longer an obscure band. The people who said "sell-out" to Dylan didn't do him any harm at all. T. Rex are twentieth-century cosmic rock stars.'

His favourite TV programmes?

'*Star Trek* – I go mad if I miss an episode – and *Catweazle*, he's an incredible character. I think that when I'm old I'll probably be just like him.'

Who cuts his hair?

'Myself.'

How does he write his songs?

'Lying in the bath.'

And what are his plans for 1971 other than scoring the next Federico Fellini movie, possibly moving to Norfolk or buying an island off Wales, publishing two books of short stories and poetry and making the next T. Rex record?

'I've just written a science-fiction film. It's already in production. It's about a character like the Silver Surfer, only a bit more ethereal, who comes to Earth to save mankind . . .'

The pencil scribbles furiously to keep pace.

'. . . like a cosmic messiah.'

FIFTEEN YEARS and over 5,000 miles from his *don't mean maybe* hollers in Marc's stacked vinyl, the 35-year-old wreckage of what once was Gene Vincent hears the half-finished hymn of some other saviour.

'Hang on to yourseeelf . . .'

There isn't much of Gene left to hang on to: an angel face sunk beneath a red fleshy sea with punchbowl eyes of morphine and Martini; a paunchy gut and a leg twice twisted in the smash of automobiles so painful it warps every nerve of body and mind; a heart eroded by four failed marriages that all failed because Gene is unmarriably insane; financial ruin, commercial obsolescence and a peptic ulcer that before the year is out will burst and send him kneeling at his mother's feet where he'll find a last ounce of strength to cough up blood and the words 'Mama, phone the ambulance now'. And that will be the screaming end of the legend they call the Screaming End.

'Come on . . .'

He hears a tune like Eddie Cochran that could break his heart if Eddie Cochran hadn't already broken it. Sweet Eddie, his rock'n'roll brother who died beside him in Gene's second accident 11 years ago. He was never the same, neither emotionally nor physically. Gene's limp, already inoperable, became a Mark of Cain he refused to have amputated. Rather hobble in crippled agony for all humanity to see what a sad and ugly world it is when life, velocity and bad luck can do *this* to a poor boy from Virginia. Let the dogs bark and the squeamish wince. Let every lurch of his deformed frame be a loud fat fuck off to the universe. America, you made him, now dare to behold your glorious black leather spastic god.

'. . . Hang on to yourseeeelf!'

Not two days ago Gene was being worshipped in England, a dying prophet self-flagellating to his last believers in the Brylcreemed shitholes of Wood Green and Southall. He's just flown home to California with a 12-hour hangover, jetlag and a writ from his fourth wife demanding child maintenance. Which is why he's come to unburden his sorrows to his manager Tom Ayres, whose Moorish mansion off Sunset has for the past five days been home to the visiting English recording artist David Bowie.

Tom is a friend of Rodney's whose moment of glory came and went producing the Sixties twist of 'Hot Pastrami' before a lucrative spell at Hanna-Barbera on *Yogi Bear* and *The Flintstones*. As well as the loan of Tom's Cadillac, David's been enjoying the hospitality of his basement recording studio and the help of a house rhythm section to make a demo of the song he first taught Mark weeks ago in Haddon Hall. Gene doesn't get David, but he gets 'Hang On To Yourself' enough to twitch a tired bone. Tom suggests it could be suitable for Gene's next album. Gene's ghost gives up something like a nod, enough to make David feel nine years old again watching *The Girl Can't Help It*. Almost. It's just the face in front of him that doesn't connect with 'Be-Bop-A-Lula'. That Gene was the face of rock'n'roll. This Gene, the face of suicide.

THE DAY DAVID ARRIVED HERE four weeks ago his new album wasn't in America's Top 200. The day he leaves, it still isn't. Four weeks of charming reporters and bewildering disc jockeys and selling himself as 'the latter-day Garbo'. But neither he nor anyone else can sell *The Man Who Sold The World*.

Not because of where David's from. The British Invasion that started in '64 hasn't stopped. Seven years later, they still can't get enough solo George and solo John, or Elton John who they gush over like he's some sort of Liberace Christ, or literally Christ if he sings like the guy from Deep Purple. Back home, the pop press crucified their own *Jesus Christ Superstar*, a rock opera concept album featuring Ian Gillan as the yodelling Son of God: in America it's now number 1, one million already sold and on its way to outselling *Sgt. Pepper* by Christmas.

But David isn't a John, Elton, George or Jesus. He's the wrong Dick Van Dyke with the wrong chim che-roos. Too much for the conservative kids of America. 'They're as conservatively hippie as their parents are conservatively straight,' he laughs. Even his new friends over at *Cashbox* agree. *'Bowie's problem stems from the fact that he is way ahead of mainstream rock.'* Way ahead of Santana, Chicago and Grand Funk Railroad. Rocking ever faster beyond the spectrum of light.

THE SLOW TRUCK BUMBLES across wet tarmac like a fat mother duck, its little cargo trailer chicks trundling behind – each stuffed with leather, nylon, parchment, Samsonite and aluminium cases, clasps and zips straining with so many shirts, boots, hats, skirts, belts, sandals, cameras, bottles, lying guidebooks, unposted postcards and hotel towels. Soon gobbled up inside the cold belly of the plane where a luggage tag for passenger Jones dangles from its handle in the darkness. Inside, unseen, a stowaway.

He breathes in dissected body parts of ink, graphite, vinyl and the pulsing creases of memory between. In two singles David picked up in Chicago by a squawking lunatic calling himself the Legendary Stardust Cowboy. In the heavenly whine of *Loaded* by The Velvet Underground. In the electric shock found in the racks of a Bay Area radio station by a group called The Stooges and the crazy tales of their singer named Iggy. In the all-seeing blink of Moondog's blind eye and the twitchy finger on a *quit-town-fag* trigger. In Ultra Violet's laugh and Gene Vincent's tears. In Kim Fowley's black heart and John Rechy's white light. In Garbo's smoke and Warhol's mirrors. In page upon page of insomniac scrawls on Holiday Inn stationery. Drawings, words, strikeouts, lyrics, names.

Zed. Eye. Gee. Gee. Why.

All of this, trembling in the turbulence at 40,000 feet, over the cowboy plains of Wyoming and Montana, a flashing speck in the sky above towns and cities glowing with evening traffic and homes cathode-bewitched by *Alias Smith and Jones*, over Saskatchewan and Manitoba, arcing above Hudson Bay and the silent emptiness of Greenland, curving over the unknowable depths of the North Atlantic, long-jumping time Pacific Coast to Greenwich Mean from night into morning, today into tomorrow. To land with a rude runway bump in a different country to the one David left 27 days ago. Where the shilling is dead and a pack of fish fingers costs 10 new pence. Where to be a member of Women's Lib is to ask the police to raid your home and the wearing of hot pants by employees of the Midland Bank a sackable offence. Where council house dreams are made of Clodagh Rodgers winning the Eurovision Song Contest and semi-detached nightmares of Ted Heath joining the Common Market.

And where Marc, in Maida Vale, sings another prayer to his cosmic messiah as David, in Beckenham, lays down his suitcase, zips open the lid and gently unpacks the bones of Ziggy Stardust.

SEVEN

ANGIE DEVOURS HIM. His New York skin and his Hollywood eyes, his Philadelphia fingers and his Chicago hips, his Detroit tongue and his Frisco groin. A travelogue of flesh now returned to her shelf and she isn't afraid to show how much she's missed its pages. The aftershock of the Earth's spin presses heavy on David's atoms as he sleepily strokes her tummy, 25 weeks' swollen. She tells him the baby's kicks have gotten stronger, just like her wildfire midnight pangs for Peking duck. But right now, her only hunger is to hear all about America.

David smiles.

America?

And sinks into oblivion.

When he wakes it is late afternoon. Kentish clouds tugboat the coming dusk, the taste of instant coffee and the faint toot of *The Magic Roundabout* over the burble of the twin-tub rinsing America from his clothes. David, home in body, is finally fully home in mind. And then he remembers.

Terry.

He's been no trouble, says Angie. He eats, he sleeps, he smokes. He goes for walks up and down the garden, from one end of the lawn across to the laurel bushes and back again, long dark coat buttoned to the collar, hands in his pockets, head tilted down with his chin on his breastbone watching the slow tread of his shoes over the grass, occasionally looking

42

up, lips tight in a silent hum, eyes wincing at the uncracked sky. But mostly he just sits quietly, like he's sitting there now, transfixed by a spotted pink cow in a sunhat chewing a daisy. Here because he wasn't sure where else to go, not after they took him out of the Cane and sent him to that other place. That's why he ran away. From *them*.

David slumps down beside him. He offers Terry a cigarette. The pink cow is arguing with an orange snail in a straw boater.

'Terry . . . you know . . .'

The cigarette is taken. David passes a light.

'You know . . . you can't stay here.'

A flame. A puff. The light is handed back.

'I know,' says Terry.

And the pink cow spins its head.

Nine miles away in Cane Hill, a nurse clicks off a television set as docile bodies shuffle to the canteen for their cold sandwich supper. In another few boings of Zebedee, Terry will be among them.

WITH A '*DHA-RRR-LING!*' FROM AMADEO and a jolly waggle of his cigarette holder. With Swiss Harry, over in his usual booth with Diamond Lil and the queens du jour, all sparkles, mascara and champagne. With Antonello, conductor at his DJ's podium, scoring the ballet of The Osmonds' 'One Bad Apple'. With Wendy, lit from the dancefloor up, in *Vogue*-fresh Ossie Clark. And with Freddie, Prince Regent of piss-elegance in his machine-fresh turquoise mandarin-collared suit. David is back where he belongs.

Sunday night at the Sombrero is as divine as he remembered and twice as colourful. A beautiful brown-skinned teenage sprite with a tight Vidal Sassoon crop dyed peroxide white spins on the floor like Twiggy in negative. A shooting star. David and Angie are smitten. Freddie and Wendy introduce her as Daniella, their 'little sister', and in a clink of fizzing glasses a happy family grows. But there's always room for one more black sheep. Even if its wool is auburn.

Freddie and Wendy know him as 'Michael'. To others he's Mickey. To his customers, he's trouble from the dark side of Half Moon Street. Mickey's trade starts with rent and ends with extortion. It's why he's three-part nerves to seven-parts speed, one eye on the nearest wallet, the other the nearest exit, manically chewing so much gum it's left a permanent crease around his mouth. But in the scarlet cinematography of the Sombrero, David is blinded by the diamond in the ruffian. A real-life Chas from *Performance*. *I like a bit of a cavort.* Another actor to add to the cast of characters slowly assembling on his mind's stage, waiting to be given their lines.

Freddie already has his. David has decided his will be the face of the new band he's been preparing with Mark and his Dulwich schoolfriends. His chosen name: the Arnold Corns. 'A bit like the Floyd's "Arnold Layne",' he reassures Mark. The boys from the band formerly known as Rungk have been busy rehearsing David's new tunes in his absence and a studio's booked to record what he hopes will be their debut single. Before a note is recorded David gallops ten thoughts ahead, sharing his vision of the Arnold Corns on stage. 'No tough tours or club appearances,' he tells Mark. 'Something like the London Palladium. The stage will be like a boxing ring with one side open to the audience. In every corner a giant super-trouper spotlight blasting at the band and flooding out into the audience. None of the coloured lights and all the rest of it. Just harsh, unforgiving white light, white heat.' He also suggests the boys from Rungk rechristen themselves with extra flamboyance. Thus, Mark, on guitar, becomes 'Mark Carr-Pritchard'. Bassist Pete de Somogyl becomes 'Polak de Somogyl'. Drummer Tim Broadbent becomes 'Timothy James Ralph St Laurent Broadbent'. And then there's Freddie, their proposed singer.

'Rudi Valentino.'

David drops the name with champagne ceremony in the Sombrero's velvet clutch. Freddie throws back his head. Wendy chokes on her bubbles.

'*Rudi Valentino?*'

'You're going to be the new Mick Jagger,' says David, grinning.

Freddie pouts juicily. 'Oh, *darling*, I told you,' he laughs, 'I *can't* sing.'

'You won't have to,' says David. 'People desire images. They like to focus on somebody who is not quite the same as them. Fantasy. Stars. *You* are an image. You *are* Rudi Valentino. You *are* a star!'

FOUR DAYS LATER, the Arnold Corns cram into the tiny basement studio of Radio Luxembourg's building in Mayfair, a dilly boy's glance round the corner from Half Moon Street. They record 'Moonage Daydream', which bobs with slow, sad Beatley steps, and the song David played for Gene Vincent, 'Hang On To Yourself', his 20-flight Cochran rocker now rumbling with added Lou Reed lyrical toughness. It is David who produces, plays piano, and sings. Freddie is nowhere to be seen. But when the record is pressed, Freddie's will be the new-Jagger-face smiling from the sleeve. In life as in *Performance*, the flashboy becomes the pop star. 'Moonage Daydream' is David Bowie disguised as the Arnold Corns pretending to be the voice of Rudi Valentino. The group is one thing, the image another.

David has just built his own Edison Lighthouse.

EYES BLASTED by Manhattan grit and Pacific sun see a new beauty in Beckenham. Springtime, and in its unhurried Kentish slumber the quaint leafy retreat he described to American disc jockeys is a picture-postcard idyll. The sap rises in an insatiable orgy of pedicels and peduncles, bracts and petals, spadices and spikelets, glumes and cymes, stamens and stigmas, catkins and corollas, anthers and pistils, miniscule nuts and bolts of organic machinery combining in a single civic engine bellowing yellows, whites, oranges, greens, pinks and violets in every tree, bush and window box. But nothing blooms in Beckenham with more colour or fertility than the music in David's head.

Every day, a fresh shoot. A scented 'Ziggy Stardust' lending mossy flesh to the bones he brought back from his travels. A delicate 'Lady Stardust'. A velvety 'Queen Bitch'. Odd cross-pollinations of Lou Reed, Kim Fowley, Sombrero sashay and a poet's observational eye. 'Changes', which pollards a musical branch from his old 'London Bye Ta-Ta'. The pansy-like 'Right On Mother', named after a recent article in the hippie magazine *Friends*. A song about 'Andy Warhol' wrapping its waxy ivy around the tune of Dylan's 'All Along The Watchtower'. And 'Quicksand', his lost postcard home from the nightmare in the cracks of the American dream. These the flowers of his bountiful new garden. But David doesn't necessarily have to pick every bouquet himself.

The climate tells him so. All down to a seed he planted just before he left for overseas, entrusting its care to his new music publisher, a chap called Bob. Bob took it to the French Riviera, to germinate in the winter sun provided by an international record and music publishing trade fair known by its French acronym, MIDEM, where pop's spymasters convene every January for six days of backhanding and champagne tremens in the beachfront shadow of Cannes' Palais des Festivals. The seed was a demo David had made, just voice and piano, of 'Oh! You Pretty Things'. Among the power brokers Bob played it to was Mickie Most, the hit producer of Lulu, Donovan and Herman's Hermits. Most is a living Midas: gold discs on his wall, a gold Rolls-Royce in his garage, a gold watch around his wrist and a gold chain around his neck from which dangle three gold-edged tiger claws. When he heard 'Oh! You Pretty Things', Most heard more gold. Exactly what he'd been looking for to launch the solo career of Peter Noone, lead 'Herman' of the Hermits, or was until he deserted them last week, scuppering all plans for an upcoming cabaret season in Caerphilly. And so David's little seed became Noone's prize carnation, or will do once Most gets him into the studio.

It refocuses David's muse. Let his music be his theatre and his songs his scripts. Let him choose the roles he thinks best for himself and let others play the parts that suit them better, just as he gave 'Moonage Daydream' to the façade of Freddie as Rudi Valentino, and now 'Oh! You Pretty Things' to Herman. Let theirs be the toothy back-page grin in *Jackie*, and he the cackling puppet master in the shadows. Become a one-man factory of song for a private family of superstars.

'It's funny how I suddenly seem to have taken off as a songwriter. But this is what living down here has done for me. I'm wrapped up in my friends and include them in the songs.'

David is sitting at his piano stool talking to a young Scottish woman from *Disc* named Rosalind. She's been sent by the paper that last year named him the 'Brightest Hope of 1970' to find out, as their editorial puts it, *'What went wrong?'* Which as far as she's seen today is mostly his wheels and his wardrobe.

Rosalind was given detailed instructions to meet David earlier today at Beckenham Junction station, vainly waiting for someone resembling the curly blond who sang 'Space Oddity' when out of nowhere popped some funny-looking lassie in a hairy blue dressing gown.

'Hi. Are you from *Disc*?'

And the penny dropped.

The ride to Haddon Hall was just as unsettling: David driving her in his boneshaker of a black Riley courtesy of a sixpence jammed in the engine to keep it spluttering over while he stopped to pick up some coffee from Sainsbury's, Rosalind gripping her loose passenger door for the whole journey convinced if she didn't it would fall off. She's since learned he calls the contraption 'Rupert' and has just written a song about it.

'Here, let me play you something.'

The words every journalist dreads, ready to unsheathe their fakest grimace.

'This is what I gave Herman.'

But for once, Rosalind is pleasantly disarmed. David sings her 'Oh! You Pretty Things', bangled hands jangling rhythmically against the keys. She agrees it sounds like a hit. Even more impressive is 'Moonage Daydream', which he plays from a vinyl acetate, encouraging Rosalind's to be the first byline to spread the gospel of the Arnold Corns and their *'incredible'* singer Rudi Valentino. As her speedy pencil shorthands down to blunt she realises David is more interested in talking about his other projects and protégés than his own records. Songs for Gene Vincent, others for the American group Three Dog Night, a single for his school friend Geoff who he says sounds like The Band's Robbie Robertson, and another for his 'art school friend' George who goes by the name 'Calvin James'. All of which David thinks will happen, none of which will, and none of which matters so long as a convincing portrait of creative industry makes print.

They step out into the garden, Rosalind admiring the stained-glass woodshed, feeling like she's walked into one of the Victorian fairy-tale illustrations framed on David's walls. Last year's 'Brightest Hope' hasn't done so badly, she thinks. So, what does he think 'went wrong'?

'I became disillusioned after "Space Oddity",' says David. 'I just decided to leave London and come to live down here.'

Here: far, far away from reality.

'I'm not bitter,' he adds. 'I was despondent at first, but all that went long ago. Really' – he fishes for unfamiliar words – 'I'm very happy.'

EIGHT

THE TEARS HANG from Marc's eyes, glistening like jewels. Tears that are neither sad nor salty, that don't run even when he shakes his curly head from side to side. Tears like the first joyful raindrops after a drought, placed on his cheeks with a dab of glue and the stroke of a finger of his wife's friend, Chelita, so that when the *Top of the Pops* cameras zoom in on his face the viewers at home will think Marc is so beautifully divine a cosmic rock messiah, he actually *cries* glitter.

It is easy to believe. He's dressed as if on shore leave from an intergalactic battleship en route to Alpha Centauri: a Mr Freedom black satin sailor top with red stars on the collar flap, golden trousers and blue suede shoes. Over his shoulder droops the strap of a Les Paul which he wields outwards from the crotch and back again like an oarsman paddling through a river of sex. The music drips with it. Pan's People skin-dive in its bliss. The critics say it sounds like something from the Fifties. But the critics are wrong, and Marc puts them right. The second single by T. Rex is Marc's *memory* of how the Fifties sounded, and, memories always being sweeter versions of reality, 'Hot Love' is the sound of the Fifties fucked senseless by the future: Elvis Presley purring 'All Shook Up' in *Barbarella*'s excessive pleasure machine. The sound of what the Seventies ought to sound like, and now can because Marc, and only Marc, has set free its true vibration. 'Hot Love' is everything its title promises for 4 minutes and 50 seconds, which is all the time it takes for the universe to finally come up to speed with Marc's ego. 'Hot Love', by T. Rex, is his first number 1.

It had to be. A country raving mad with hot pants fever craves a new national anthem. 'Hot Love' is it: the symphonic wiggle of a peachy behind in satin, suede, stretch jersey, denim or Terylene. *Uh-huh-huh.* Marc sees it for himself the first time they play the song on *Top of the Pops.*

'The little girls were dancing away in their little hot pants and that really turned me on.'

Not just little girls but big girls, short girls, tall girls, all girls. John Lewis girls allowed to sell them but not wear them. Peek Freans girls sent home by their bosses for dressing inappropriately while boxing custard creams. Hull girls who strip Hammonds department store of its first delivery in 48 hours. Posh girls banned from sporting them at Ascot by the Duke of Norfolk. German girls invading London where the Fräulein Hot Pants contest is being held in homage to the city where the craze first started. Desperate Croydon girls weeping ink to *Rave* magazine: *'How can I persuade my mother to let me wear hot pants? I'm 15 and very slim and I saved up to buy a pair which I think look great – but when I put them on my mother nearly had a fit and says I've got to take them back to the shop. Why is mum so old-fashioned?'* Never in human history has a nation been so divided by the combined might of fabric and the female rump.

The radio yells 'Power To The people', but the kids don't care and Lennon's fist pumps only as far as number 7. That's why 'Hot Love' – the *real* revolution – is number 1. A revolution in sound, fashion, sex and mind. The council house Cinders of Britain are going to the ball in hot pants whether their mothers like it or not. No one can stop them now T. Rex have released their inner woman of gold. Boys too, now twopenny-princes wide awake with fresh purpose skulk to the Boots counter for something other than Clearasil. Today, just two drops of glitter: tomorrow, a sparkling monsoon. The Communists needed a manifesto. The kids of '71 need only *'La la la, la-la-la-la'.* 'Hot Love' is the revolution, all right. The record doesn't have to spell it out but given a live mic on *Top of the Pops,* Marc doesn't waste the moment.

'*Groove Rev-o-luuu-tion!'*

And so it begins.

The workers march against anti-union legislation in the biggest public demonstration in peacetime.

The women march for equal pay, equal education and equal opportunities.

The gays march for a world where nobody needs to place *Time Out* personals reading:

> **Gay professional guy**, 33 (North London) seeks an attractive girl in her early 20s (preferably gay herself) to take out occasionally so that he can create a 'straight' image for himself in the right places. All expenses paid and about 85p per hour.

The Tory Monday Club, not marching but sneering, stone the 'unnecessary' Welfare State: 'The lower levels don't need so much income because they don't need books or tickets to the theatre.'

The bookish lower levels of the Angry Brigade commit to violent retribution. 'WE ARE READY TO GIVE OUR LIVES FOR LIBERATION.'

On placards, in pickets, in anarchist communiqués and homemade bombs, all fences collapse leaving Britons nowhere to sit. Pop papers run fashion ads for swastika arm bands 'only £1.25' and Rod Stewart declares that 'Enoch Powell is a good thing'. Enoch says uniting with Europe is a bad thing and finds another pop star ally in the pages of *Disc*. 'The people should be fighting against the Common Market, but they won't until it's too late,' says last year's 'Brightest Hope' David Bowie. 'Britain just doesn't know what revolution is.'

Oh, David. Can't you *hear*?

WHAT MUSIC! If it *is* music. A sensory assault of note upon note, repeating yet not quite repeating, the same, yet not exactly the same, as if forever frantically trying to escape itself only to arrive right back at its point of origin. Music you don't listen to so much as submit to like an insurmountable polyphonic checkmate. Music with no romance but absolute feeling, scored by cold concrete and metal streetlights on a midnight cab fare to the Bronx. *Music In Similar Motion.* The music of Philip Glass.

The Royal College of Art has heard nothing like it. Neither had Wimbledon College of Art two nights earlier when Glass and his ensemble played the first of their low-key performances in London, organised at the last minute on his way home after touring the continent with fellow New York experimental composer Steve Reich. Neither art school gig is advertised in the press and the only review is that in an academic journal written by one of Reich's own English musicians. '*A flowing music of quite beautiful resonance and richness,*' writes 26-year-old Michael Nyman, speaking to a world too nervous to listen. No concert hall is willing to book Glass, and until they do loft spaces, galleries and colleges like these are his only option.

The audience is not big. Art students, their friends, hippies, freaks, those lacking the ticket or soul to see James Brown over the road in the Albert Hall, those wanting more from a Wednesday night than Ena Sharples and *Softly, Softly*. Those like 22-year-old Brian from an artists' co-op in Camberwell, who in Glass hears the jet engines starting on his own roxy musical airplane ride. And maybe – because why not? – in another corner, another pair of ears shredded by the same volley of amplified voices, strings and electronic keyboards tremble under flowing long hair? *No, surely not?* Is that *him* in the blue fur coat? Are those Peruvian wedding bangles? Would history dare to be *this* contrived?

Is that really *you*, David?

HE DRIVES THROUGH LEWISHAM with a tune in his head, but it sounds nothing like Philip Glass. More like the Rolling Stones' 'Let's Spend The Night Together'.

'*Beep! Beep!*'

The song is 'Rupert The Riley'. David's just been working on a demo with Mark, taping sound effects of his black Riley RM speeding down Southend Road with the exhaust silencer off. Only today 'Rupert', the song, is running a lot steadier than Rupert the bloody car. Turning a corner into Ladywell Road, the steering wheel begins to judder in his hands. A strange noise from the engine. Maybe he needs to jiggle that sixpence? He sees a parking space up ahead. The noise again. Shifting gears, he turns into the kerb. The vehicle splutters a low bronchial mechanical gurgle. Then ominous silence.

David reaches below his seat with a resigned sigh, pulling out a long metal handle bent at right angles. He climbs out, carrying it to the front of the car where he screws it into a hole in the grille above the bumper. He gives it a sharp crank clockwise. Nothing.

Another crank.

Mocking deathly inertia.

So he cranks again . . .

''ERE, COME AND HAVE A LOOK AT THIS!'

The officer calls without shifting his gaze from the window of Lewisham Police Station. A second officer sidles up behind him, peering over his shoulder. He sees it too.

'Ho-ho! What a Charlie!'

Another bobby joins them, all three now chuckling at the pantomime of a queer-looking bloke with long hair huffing and puffing trying to start his big old-fashioned spiv's car. The more he cranks, the funnier he looks. Hair flapping, face reddening, the engine refusing to cough into life.

Ho, ho!

Turn after turn, nothing happening.

Ha, ha!

Redder and redder, sillier and sillier.

Hee, hee!

Just look at him, cranking and cranking.

Ho, ho!

And the car not budging.

Ha, ha!

And then it jumps forward squashing the daft bugger against the car parked in front.

. . . Oh?!

THE CRANK that was in David's hand is now embedded in David's leg. It got there the moment he realised, too late, that he'd left Rupert in gear. The same moment the engine finally turned over and – in a blink – the vehicle sprang into motion, transforming the handle into a bayonet, stabbing his thigh and narrowly missing both his thin femoral artery and his considerably fatter penis. Blood spurts from the tear in his trousers where the shaft protrudes, still attached to the grille pinning his knees between bumpers. He screws his eyes shut. And screams like he's never screamed before.

When he opens them again, he's staring at three ashen policemen.

THE HOSPITAL is only around the corner. In less than an hour, David is stitched up and lying in a men's ward where he must remain for observation. The doctors tell him he's been very lucky: had he sliced the artery he could have bled to death. And like being stabbed all over again the realisation sends him dizzy. His head sinks back on his pillow, eyes lost in some invisible infinity beyond the gloomy sash windows. Outside, where life goes on in a world the flavour of Instant Whip, and where Marc Bolan and his unpunctured thighs groove on, forever it seems, at number 1.

NINE

MARC CANNOT SAVE HER. Nobody can. Life has lost all meaning, even in a world of 'Hot Love', which is all the world she knows. Marc's world is *her* world, smiling into the lens of a BBC camera on the *Top of the Pops* studio floor, picked out as one of the prettier audience 'dancing dollies', blonde hair, slinky hips and sexy boots. Nobody ever asks her age, and if they do Samantha never tells them she's only 15. Nor when older men who tell her she's 'beautiful' ask if she'd like to join them afterwards for a drink. The world where she is loved and treated as a woman. Up there, among the stars. But when you're thrown up that high, the fall to the bedroom of a Watford semi can kill. And it does.

It is a Monday night when Samantha sits at her dressing table, the two bottles of barbiturates she's stolen from her mother's drawer sitting next to her open red leatherette diary. She is crying as she writes.

> *Don't laugh at me for being dramatic but I really just can't take any more. All anyone has ever done is tell me what a problem I am. I am just a dreamer and none of my dreams will ever come true. I just can't face reality. I wish someone would really love me. I always give the impression that I am well-bred and overflowing with confidence, but it is so false. I sit and*

dream for hours as a fairy godmother and see me as a star or as Sinatra's wife. But it is all dreams. I have got some of mummy's own pills. I don't know what they are, but I am going to eat all of them, and I am going to eat bread to get it all down (bet it bloody doesn't work).

I know it's awful and I am being very, very selfish, but I'm sick of being told how selfish I am. God bless.

X X X

Her mother finds the body.

The police take Samantha's diary as evidence for the inquest. In it, they read what her mother had read with alarm a few weeks earlier when she'd found it while cleaning, a discovery which led to the tearful argument banning her daughter from ever going back to *Top of the Pops*. Tales of being wooed by a Radio 1 disc jockey and spending the night in his bed under the spell of dreamy pills to help her relax.

The papers smell scandal. Redtop horror stories describe a *Top of the Pops* 'SLAVE MARKET' of nubile flesh. The BBC quickly quench the flames with the wet scoffs of regular host Jimmy Savile. 'I've met young crumpet that would knock your eyes out,' he calmly reassures the *Mirror*. 'Fourteen-year-olds with bodies on 'em like Gina Lollobrigida. I love 'em, but not in the going-to-bed sense. I have a laugh with 'em. A cup of tea and a chat.' The 44-year-old DJ who last month the *NME* named *'the Peter Pan of pop'* surely would not lie.

Hertfordshire constabulary concur that Samantha's diary is 'quite worthless': the inquest dismisses it as inadmissible fantasy. 'It would be ridiculous to connect anyone or anything mentioned in her diary with reality,' says the senior investigating officer. The coroner's verdict: 'suicide while the balance of her mind was disturbed'.

Samantha's diary is 'mislaid' and never returned to her mother. Lost forever, like its author, snatched from a world where Jimmy Savile takes tea with his crumpet and Marc Bolan grooves on, forever it seems, at number 1.

★

BUT THERE IS ANOTHER WORLD where he isn't. Marc finds it in New York's Lower East Side the week after Easter. A world where The Temptations are number 1 and 'Hot Love' not yet in the Top 100, where Marc can walk through Times Square unmolested by teenage girls, and T. Rex are bottom of the bill at the Fillmore East below a Christian rocker called Mylon and the heavy torture of Mountain. It is Marc's second tour of the States, though his first with his Byronic rogue of a conga tickler Mickey Finn in tow, the handsome duo now all the mightier for the extra amplification of a bass player from Grimsby named Steve and a drummer from Essex named Bill. A might which is bitterly wasted on the stonewashed ears of the gum-dumb Fillmore crowd. This is not Fairfield Halls in Croydon, where weeks ago the ceiling ricocheted with 'MARC!' from a screeching choir of unquenchable menstrual energy. This is a dead denim abattoir refusing to admit that Woodstock ended two years ago. Squinting through the borderlights, Marc sees their mocking sniggers. He flicks the hair from his eyes, pulls the microphone close, and shares his thoughts.

'Instead of *you* cunts, we could be at home playing to people who *want* to see us!'

The battle is lost. A cacophonous 'Hot Love' gains a ripple of applause but when they leave the stage it's without the echoing Godspeed of a single whoop. In the back of the hall, the woman from *Billboard* magazine is vexed. *'Very strange indeed and very loud,'* she decides: their rhythms *'idiotic'*, Marc's songs *'simple-minded'*. But there aren't enough young Yankees in hot pants to disagree with her. 'Hot Love' will only reach America's number 72.

Back in his Midtown hotel room, Marc rages. Yesterday, he'd calmly told a journalist if the States didn't dig T. Rex then that was 'cool'. Tonight, he wants cold-blooded revenge. His only weapon, his guitar, which he snatches into his lap, thrashing the strings in a hot adrenaline ecstasy, every follicle on his head a bouncing black antenna ready to receive the next cosmic transmission.

It comes.

Not a song yet, just a vibe. The sort you don't find while soaking in the bath in Maida Vale, only here in the '71 New York twilight chaos of three-buck heroin bags, hustlers, gypsies, tramps, thieves and freaks too cool for the Fillmore already in bands called Suicide, out there hissing in the Downtown darkness playing what in '71 Gotham they already advertise as 'Punk Music'. Like Marc's, the lick of a tetchy New York of fuckoff and screwyou and suckmydick, telling a crowdofcunts they ain't even as hip as motherfucking Croydon.

'YE-AH!'

A hot vamp like a vampire sucking the neon nightblood out of mad bad Manhattan. A tune that sounds like cheap sex for cheap money and worth every grubby cent. Dirty and sweet. Marc screams for joy.

'OW-UH!'

He feels the burning caress of the rock'n'roll gods whisper their abracadabra in his ear. And sings.

'GET – IT – ON!'

FIVE MONTHS BEHIND AMERICA and one year past its sell-by date, *The Man Who Sold The World* by David Bowie is released in a land still bopping, forever it seems, to Marc Bolan at number 1. At £2 and 15 new pence the album is a perverse luxury equivalent to over 200 Findus fish fingers, three dozen tins of Heinz baked beans, or 20 boxes of Quaker Sugar Puffs. Britons will not go hungry for want of 'All The Madmen'. Not when it comes housed in a new sleeve whose very purpose is to spoil the appetites of every red-blooded hod carrier who likes their meat with two veg and their music without the visual accessory of a girly-looking bloke in a dress lying on a chaise longue, tossing playing cards on the carpet like some crazy version of patience.

David, out of hospital, feels no less crippled by the album than he does by the limp from his injury, which, like many of its tracks, hangs around longer than he'd prefer. 'There was nothing ambitious about *The Man Who Sold The World*, except maybe the ambition to crawl out of a cave,' he says, gamely going through the motions of trying to sell it to the handful of reporters prepared to spare him their pencil lead. Most are more interested in the lavish clothes on the cover than the lumpy songs within. 'It's purely decorative,' explains David of his latest incarnation as Greta Geezer of Beckenham. 'Just theatre.'

The editor of *Melody Maker*, circulation 145,000, refuses to run an offending photo of the new feminine David beside the interview.

The editor of the *Mirror*, circulation 4 million, isn't so prudish. David, in his dress, makes the same Saturday pop pages that two months ago outed Lionel Bart. 'I get all sorts of abuse showered on me,' he tells them over lunch of chicken salad and vodka in Haddon Hall, served by a heavily pregnant Angie, relishing her role as a bawdy mascot of straight domesticity. 'It doesn't worry me anymore what people say. I get called a queer and all sorts of things. But my sexual life is normal.' It does nothing for sales of *The Man Who Sold The World*, though it does wipe the slate of David's tired old public image. No more 'the "Space Oddity" guy': now 'that queer feller in the dress'.

In its aftermath, in the plugging trenches beyond Fleet Street, the ever-industrious Anya braves a trip to the fortress of the BBC in White City, armed with a copy of the LP and a press release describing David as 'thoroughly rounded', listing his musical influences as Stravinsky, Vaughan Williams, Dvořák, Elgar and Holst, his words indebted to Albert Camus, Harold Pinter, Brendan Behan, Keith Waterhouse, John Rechy and Oscar Wilde. What any of these have to do with a song like 'She Shook Me Cold' isn't clear, not that the *Top of the Pops* producer Anya doorsteps to pitch David for the show's current 'album slot' will get as far as removing the vinyl from its dust jacket.

'*David Bowie?*'

He thrusts the LP back at her – 'We don't have perverts on this show!' – and with a gentle shove sends her stumbling out of his office, then slams the door.

Anya picks *The Man Who Sold The World* off the floor where it just dropped, David still smiling coyly on the back in his Garbo beret. Isn't it just as he'd told the *Mirror*?

'I cannot breathe in the atmosphere of convention. I find freedom only in the realms of my own eccentricity.'

Just so. Tucking it snugly under her arm, she walks away, her strides defiant, down the suffocating corridors of the great British Broadcasting Corporation. Where suited men with trimmed moustaches and tie pins sit in boardrooms discussing the latest viewing figures of *The Dick Emery Show*, laughing about their star's hilarious turn as 'Mandy' in a blonde wig and stuffed blouse, swinging a pink handbag. Stainless of all sins involving popular disc jockeys and eye-popping young crumpet.

Nobly protecting the nation from the scourge of perverts on *Top of the Pops*.

THE MIRACLE OF THE YOUNG MAN everyone still calls 'Herman' is that at the age of 23 Peter Noone isn't yet insane. Maybe it's because, as he says, 'I'm still basically a kid . . . a spoilt little bastard sometimes, too!' A big kid with a big face that is 90 per cent teeth, with eyes that could break your grandma's heart and a jaw that could break your grandpa's walnuts, still beaming boyishly on the front cover of *Fabulous 208* and the back cover of *Mirabelle*, in spite of all fame has thrown at him. At 14, Noone was on TV screens in *Coronation Street*. At 16, he was number 1 in the British charts as singer with Herman's Hermits, a band he only joined because his dad acted as guarantor for all their gear bought on tick. At 17, he was number 1 in America. At 18, he'd had the starring role in two film musicals by MGM. At 19, he was an alcoholic millionaire on a bottle of vodka a day. At 23, Peter Noone might have ended up horizontal in a pool of meths, crying to the rats in his skip about the time he used to be 'Enery the Eighth, he was. Instead, he's wound up as *Tailor & Cutter*'s 'Best Dressed Man' of 1971, living in a luxury Knightsbridge flat furnished with silver candelabras and gold carriage clocks, with a Yorkshire terrier called Mickey and a glamorous French wife called Mireille. And her parents.

Squeaky clean and soda sober, Peter has replaced the drinks cabinet with the stock market. His daily paper: the *Financial Times*. His toilet reading: a guide to Swiss banking. The notepad by his phone: to record his daily sales figures. But now that the Hermits have stopped selling, Herman has to reconsider his options.

'Peter's got to make the change,' agrees his gold-plated producer, Mickie Most. 'He can't sing clap-hands songs like "Mrs Brown, You've Got A Lovely Daughter" all the time.' Most hasn't let Peter down yet. If he tells him now is the time to go solo, Peter goes solo. And if he tells him he's found 'the perfect song' to relaunch him, Peter agrees. 'Oh! You Pretty Things' is 'perfect'.

David is invited along to the recording session in Holborn to play the piano part Most liked from his original demo, accompanied by his old friend Herbie on bass, and Clem Cattini on drums – the same rhythm section as Clive Dunn's 'Grandad'. Peter assumes the song has been written specially for him. David doesn't shatter the illusion. Why tell him he wrote it with half a mind on Nietzschean philosophy and the Nazis, the other thinking about his unborn child, his mad brother Terry and the bright lights of the Sombrero. Not when Peter genuinely seems to believe David is 'the new Paul McCartney' – possibly because, as few critics miss, 'Oh! You Pretty Things' sounds a lot like The Beatles' 'Martha My Dear'.

Peter sings David's words sweetly, if with the lyrical grasp of a slow child forced to stand up in class and read aloud Shakespeare who then sits back down again without the foggiest as to what just happened. Most's tiger claw necklace dangles Midasly over the mixing desk as he pushes faders, making that all-important change in Peter's career by underpinning the tune with a beat even the deaf would reasonably describe as the 'clap-hands' variety. The result: a jolly wheeltap and shunt the artist formerly known as Herman should be able to perform in his regular guest slot on the BBC's new Friday night Mike Yarwood show without anyone at home suffering a stroke.

Before the session is over, they manage to record one more of David's songs, 'Right On Mother', its sound just as chipper and its hook even better suited to Peter's innate George Formby whine. Most is so impressed he tries to persuade David to make a whole album with Peter. 'A concept LP,' he suggests, 'with each song linked to the next.' Peter thinks it's a brilliant idea. 'David's a terrific songwriter,' he later raves to *Mirabelle*. 'But it's a shame. He doesn't really want to be a singer. He just wants to be successful by letting other people sing his songs . . .'

FOR THE SIXTH WEEK RUNNING, Marc Bolan is number 1. Then, in a skank out of nowhere, he isn't. 'Hot Love' by T. Rex is finally knocked off the top by Jamaica's Dave & Ansil Collins. 'Double Barrel' was recorded over a year ago but only now, in the late spring of '71, does its bootlaced beat connect in a land where Enoch Powell's majority is audibly weakening. Unprepared for overnight success, the Collinses are flown over to promote the single. The fame they enjoy, but not the cold English weather, nor the even colder English girls. 'I need sex day and night,' complains Ansil, who becomes so dangerously unsatiated he begs *Record Mirror* to be sent back to the beauties of Kingston as soon as he can. 'To unload myself.'

Fully loaded and half-finished, Marc is still in the States when he learns that the reign of 'Hot Love' is over, if too many spins of the planet ahead on his fretboard to care. Fresh from Los Angeles, he's spit-polished his new titanium groove, 'Get It On', recorded a shooting star's throw from Hollywood Boulevard. Now he's in another studio back in New York, rockabillying yet more galactic voodoo called 'Jeepster'. His wing man – and formerly David's – Tony Visconti has been with him most of the trip, producing T. Rex on the hoof between a holiday visit to his folks in Brooklyn. America may not have warmed to Marc but, as the tape reels in Tony's return luggage testify, its glitterless apathy has set his muse gloriously ablaze. The payback is all there in acetylene riffs and Casanova jive. Marc boards his flight to London having seen and not conquered a land he no longer deems worthy of conquering. Heading home, in gong-banging glory, to the one he already has.

TEN

SEE THE GIRLS OF SUMMER. Dirty and sweet, windy and wild, flipping hips and sliding bones. 'Girls are sexier now,' a physician tells an international medical conference in London and the pavements of Kensington do not lie. The darling buds of the first Saturday in May skip traffic lights fantastic. Taxi horns beep sonnets and radios sizzle with drooling suitors. *How cum ya taste so goooood?* The fashion mags answer. *'Because girls are beginning to look like girls again and although we sympathise with Women's Lib, we don't believe you have to look like a feller to get equal rights!'* The factory shut and the office silent, today, they know, the city is theirs. All that hell of servitude for all this heaven of style.

Heaven, by address, number 120 Kensington High Street. Biba! *'The Mecca for dollies,'* say the papers. Art deco temple of potted palms and ostrich feathers where they walk in as Mary and walk out Marlene. Threads much too pretty for metal rails, hung from hat stands, works of art for girls who believe, as Oscar said, one should either be one or wear one, and who come to Biba to achieve both. Enemies of nothing and nobody except dowdiness and the working week. Suddenly caught in the fools' crossfire.

BLOW IT UP OR BURN IT DOWN!

62

The bomb detonates at peak trading. Nobody is killed. Two phone calls to the manager – a nine-minute warning, then a five – are long enough to evacuate the building of over 500 shoppers and 70 staff. The only injury, a security guard thrown 25 feet by the blast in the basement; the only real damage, to stock, fixtures and lost profits. For the sinister spectre of the Angry Brigade, mission accomplished.

> The only thing you can do with modern slave-houses — called boutiques — IS WRECK THEM. You can't reform profit capitalism and inhumanity. Just kick it till it breaks.
> Revolution.

And so a war that started in January trying to assassinate Tory cabinet ministers is reduced to the scalps of moss crepe dresses.

But the anarchists chose poorly. Biba began as designer Barbara Hulanicki's dream to make elegant clothes affordable to all. Her philosophy: to create a new kind of store where girls can come and look in wonder without being intimidated into buying anything. Rule number one: any assistant who asks 'Can I help you?' is sacked on the spot. Biba is a business, but its capital is beauty. Kick it in vain – beauty will *always* kick back.

Not 50 yards down the same side of Kensington High Street, the real revolution continues – at 45 a minute on the floor of the Sombrero, where the only bombers among the too-beautiful-to-be-angry brigade are the black ones coursing through their bloodstream.

Through the superbad hustle David sees the sultan of sulphate, Half Moon Street Mickey, wetly smacking gum, smiling back at him with an odd look of shared triumph. *Poor Michael.* Last week David thought it would be a riot to coax him into a recording studio and make him sing 'Rupert The Riley'. The shock being it wasn't nearly as painful as being stabbed in the thigh with a spinning crankshaft. Mickey – alias 'Sparky King' as David announces him in the pages of *Beat Instrumental* – blagged it as a singer like he blags every greasy pound note that slips through his fingers. Just a shame no A&R man who hears 'Rupert The Riley' is stupid enough to want a novelty record about an old banger that sounds like the Stones ruining the theme to *Here Come the Double Deckers!* No matter who sings it.

But down here, who cares? It's all just another scream, dear. A biblical flood could pour down the stairs and they'd drown admiring their own reflections. The world *up there* can blow itself to bits with its silly bombs and angry manifestos. Turn up the music, Antonello! More champagne, Juanito! No explosions will ever stop *these* girls of summer. Dirtier and sweeter, windier and wilder, flipping such hips and sliding – oh, *what* bones! Darling David – smashing riah for an omi – sailing across the floor in the big kaffies Freddie made specially for him. And Angie – why, isn't she *bold*? – eight months gone but jiving defiant like a piece of string with a knot in the middle. And Freddie, now vada *her*, all dolly in lilac – *lovely* shade – and Daniella like a bijou Indian princess twinkling beside him. And Wendy, dancing in her own cloud of stardust looking simply *fantabulosa* and – ah! – well she would, wouldn't she, dear? She's wearing Biba.

THE SONGS KEEP COMING. Good ones. Better than 'Rupert The Riley' and too good to waste on rent boys called Sparky. Songs David would rather record himself. If he had his own band to play them.

He can't ignore it any longer. *The Man Who Sold The World* is already dead, all the deader because he can't play any gigs to promote it because the band who made it no longer exists. Its unexpectedly encouraging reviews plague him with their collective praise: *Time Out* for *'Tony Visconti's mean, stalking, persistent bass'*; dear Rosalind in *Disc* picking out *'Mick Woodmansey on drums'*; and her pop ladyship Penny Valentine, now at *Sounds*, in an electric lather over *'some ferocious guitar work from Mick Ronson'*. All of them, now gone: Tony on the high road to 'Hot Love', Mick and Woody on the low road to Hull.

David could, if he wished, still play solo acoustic shows, only, as he tells the *Maker*, he's sick and tired of the club scene.

'I prefer to work with a proscenium arch.'

Performance! Not *a* stage but *The* Stage. The type of stage where he saw his first rock'n'roll show, aged 9, Tommy Steele rattling the loggia boxes of the Finsbury Park Empire with the hits written especially for him by his homosexual communist junkie friend Lionel. Or the mock-Gothic splendour of the Woolwich Granada where, aged 15, David watched Little Richard scandalise its stage with his awopboppin' raptures and black queen burlesque. *Rock'n'roll theatre.*

He needs not a band, but a troupe. Players in every sense who can act out the dramas in his head in front of an audience, learning his lines, following his cues, and costumed according to his instructions. There are plenty of musicians he'd like to cast, all of them spoken for. Terry Cox, who drummed on 'Space Oddity', now in Pentangle. Rick Wakeman, still in David's phone book as a studio pianist but, for now, committed to the Strawbs. Herbie Flowers, too loyal to Blue Mink and already spread far too thinly as a session bassist. Which leaves him only Mark across the road, a solid guitar player he can always rely on. But Mark still wants to write and sing his own songs and there's no room for two authors in the Bowie folio. He needs fresh malleable talent. 'Most musicians today are boring because they have no sense of stage presence,' he mulls. 'They're more concerned with music and writing rather than any stagecraft. They prefer to have a sense of sympathy with the audience, and to *be* another member of the audience, which reduces the impact of being any form of celebrity or star.' David *is* a star, he knows. All he needs is the right band to make it shine.

A **MORRIS 1000** pulls up outside Haddon Hall. Out step two guns for hire gazing uneasily at the Hammer horror film façade marking the end of a tiring drive down from the North.

They've come here on David's request, as recommended by his old producer friend Gus Dudgeon. Ritchie Dharma, a drummer from Leicester via Manchester where his parents run an Indian takeaway. And Rick Kemp, a bass player – from Hull. Until a few months ago they were the pluck and thud accompanying East Riding warbler Michael Chapman, which is how Gus knows them. Rick met Chapman while he was working in the music department of Hammonds on Paragon Square. It was Rick who first told Chapman about a mercurial local guitarist named Mick Ronson, and thanks to Rick that Mick was asked to play with them on one of Chapman's albums, produced by Gus. The slimmest degree of separation, yet they've been sent to David without any coercion from Mick himself, who neither have spoken to in over a year.

Rick and Ritchie's M1-weary buttocks greet the banquette seating of David's front room with silent agony. David, in one of his Mr Fish's, makes himself comfortable on the carpet. He asks them questions while betraying an impression of already knowing all the answers about who they've worked with and what they've done. Just one or two curious blanks to fill.

'Kemp?' he asks. 'Are you related to Lindsay Kemp?'

'Not that I'm aware,' says Rick.

'Oh,' says David, and quietly lights another Dunhill.

An hour passes without playing one note of the music he's been working on, nor does he ask either of them for a practical demonstration of their own musical ability. This is not an audition, they realise, more an informal assessment of vibe compatibility. All that way for a pleasant if abstract conversation with a living Botticelli painting, wasted petrol money and a sore arse.

David waves them off from his doorstep. They wave back, smiling, as the car pulls into Southend Road, heading northwards.

'Well?' says Ritchie.

'Lovely bloke,' sighs Rick. 'But I really can't see him doing anything ever again, can you? I don't think he even knows which way the wind's blowing, does he?'

BUT DAVID DOES KNOW. He'd know even if the critics didn't keep telling him, which they do. Five weeks after Penny first told him in *Sounds*, the *Maker* finally get round to reviewing *The Man Who Sold The World*. There it is again. *'Mick Ronson plays excellent lead guitar . . .'* David hears, loud and clear. *'. . . an epic quality . . .'* His songs and Mick's strings: the light

66

and the prism. '. . . *there are some tremendous flashes of brilliance here. Explore.*' If only they could.

Oh, Mick! All that colour. All those shapes. And look at you now . . .

IT HURT TO SEE HIM. Only last week, on stage in a basement club off Chinatown nicknamed 'the speed palace', bottom of a Friday night bill of heavy noise with a band that *Time Out* don't even bother listing. Mick's own band, which is why they're called Ronno. Which is the first but least of their problems.

Ronno are the scab of the wound when Mick left David: the congealed blood of the band that were once Hull's the Rats, then David's Hype and Harry The Butcher, now a zombified Rats again in all but inadvisable name. Their lifeline had been the deal Angie helped secure them last year with Philips when still Hype, when still Mick, Tony on bass and Woody newly on drums. After Mick and Woody deserted David, back in Hull they reconvened with their old Rats singer, Benny. With Tony producing and still filling in as bassist they made one single for Vertigo – Philips' alternative rock imprint for the likes of Black Sabbath – a song Tony suggested by an all but unknown American singer he'd been working with named Tucker Zimmerman, '4th Hour Of My Sleep'. The *Maker* called it a *'hot little reminder of a Beatles song'*, which was true in a forgettable 'Ballad Of John And Yoko' kind of fashion. It would be Ronno's first and last review in the national press.

Twelve weeks later, the last sands of time slipping through their fingers, Mick invites David to witness Ronno in the patchouli gloom of the Temple club where they've been offered the opening slot on a Vertigo showcase night. The headliners are a tartan prog dirge called Beggar's Opera who've chosen to reimagine the works of nineteenth-century Austro-Hungarian composers through the modern sorcery of electromagnetic amplification, an art for which their guitarist, Ricky, will one day suffer badly. Below them, the fiddly fretboard sweat of Black August. And then Ronno, a dead zeppelin rotting in a riffs' graveyard three years and two beards behind the times.

Oh, Christ! *Mick?* Didn't you *read* David's thoughts on 'heavy rock' the other week in *Sounds*?

'I think it's fairly primitive as a musical form. I look for sensation rather than quality, and heavy music seems to be full of musicians who have quality rather than musicians who for some reason can chill your spine.'

But there you are, Mick, on stage with all your quality and not a note of sensation, paddling your Gibson up shit metal creek. Because Hull has deafened you again. Blinded you with its suicide skies and its flat-earthed faces, its white phone boxes no superhero will ever burst from to save you. Turned you into what you think you need to be in order to survive a city where venereal disease is local front-page news in a paper that blames it all on *Get Carter*. All that power in your prism, and no rainbows to split, no light to dapple. Just loud, ugly darkness.

But in the darkness, David sees. And through the squeals, David hears. The frets of a golden Les Paul, discreetly tapping an SOS.

A WEEK PASSES. And then he acts. The front door closes on a Morris 1000 vanishing into the distance and a nicotine-yellow forefinger pokes the circular hole on a plastic dial and twists it clockwise.

0. *Whir-r-r-r-r-r-r-r-r!*

4. *Whir-r-r-r!*

8. *Whir-r-r-r-r-r-r!*

2. *Whir-r!*

Copper wires buzz with electric current travelling 160 miles in less than a heartbeat. Exchanges connect sending voltage just strong enough to ring the bell inside the telephone in number 8 Milton Grove. The ringing stops when a hand picks up the plastic receiver and a circuit is completed.

A female voice says, 'Hello?'

A carbon granule microphone condenses.

A male voice says, 'Can I speak to Mick?'

Diaphragms fluctuate.

'Who's calling, please?'

Coils vibrate.

'It's David.'

Rocking armatures rock.

'Just one moment . . .'

Mrs Ronson gently places the receiver beside the phone and shouts up from the foot of the stairs.

'Mick . . . Phone for you . . . it's David.'

Let there be light.

WHEN HE WALKS through the door of Haddon Hall it feels like yesterday. A slightly different yesterday, the rooms flipped around, the colours not quite as he remembered, but the time-warping ageless energy of an inescapably eternal past the same. David is first to hug him. Then Angie, rushing forward and throwing her arms around his back – 'MICK!' – squeezing him as much as her protruding belly will allow.

'COME UPSTAIRS!'

She leads him up the hall staircase to the square-shaped first-floor landing to nowhere, sealed off from the flats on either side rented by the Charles and Adams families. 'The mezzanine level,' Angie jokes. Mick sees a mattress behind the banister.

'Hope you like your new bedroom.'

Mick's first evening back with David is spent in the music room, the front room, their bedroom, all over the house listening to his new songs, live on piano and guitar, or on taped demo reels. Hearing the light, Mick's head begins arranging the colours: make that one more brown, add a red line there, darken that bridge part. But the light itself is blinding. Mick is overwhelmed by the intensity, every tune a white-hot melodic blast unique from the next. 'Lady Stardust', 'Bombers', 'Andy Warhol'. All of them, solid proper *songs*.

David has his first show of the year in a couple of weeks, a BBC radio concert for John Peel, just like Mick's first gig with him last year. He needs his help to form a new band. David will sing and play guitar and piano. He has Mark across the road who can play rhythm guitar, and he might be able to rope Herbie in again on bass. But he needs a drummer. Mick takes the hint.

'I'll ask Woody,' he says. 'And there's always Trev.'

Trevor Bolder. David didn't take a lot of notice of him when he saw Ronno, just a beard and a Slag Brothers haircut shaking over a Fender Mustang in the deep end of cacophony. When Mick and Woody returned to Hull, they needed someone local to replace Tony, only ever their studio bass player, anchored to his work life in London. Trevor was the last bass player in Hull they hadn't already tried and the best they ever had. A jobbing hairdresser, piano tuner and, like his father, champion trumpeter, Trevor's musical bones are understretched on four strings. Like so much in Hull, this is a secret yet to be shared with the outside world.

'So you, Woody and Trev,' says David. 'You mean just use Ronno?'

Just use Ronno. And with these three words, though Mick doesn't know it yet, nor Woody, nor Trevor, nor their poor singer Benny, unaware he's about to be marooned on the bitter shores of couldabeen, Ronno – *hallelujah!* – are no more.

UNTIL THEN, David still has his *other* playthings. The Arnold Corns' single is out, though not yet their mischievous secret. 'Nothing is really new – the twentieth century has nothing to offer,' he bugles. 'At least "Moonage Daydream" is unique – there is nothing to compare it with.' David rallies the papers to attention, maintaining the charade of being only their writer and producer while proudly introducing the universe to the band's real star – a human phenomenon destined, he swears, for number 1 in the charts and the cover of *Vogue* – 'Rudi Valentino'.

The universe isn't ready, but here he comes, bolting out of the Sombrero and onto the newsstands like a frisky genie spouting free from his lamp in eyeshadow, foundation and silver-streaked hair. *'He's 19 years old and staggering,'* wobbles a predisposed Penny Valentine. *'He's very, very pretty and deliberately funny, very open and genuine, somehow very vulnerable. You can't help liking him.'* Most of the girls agree he looks 'astonishingly' like Mick Jagger. Except over in *Mirabelle*, where 'HE'S THE DISHIEST BOY IN TOWN' and the office consensus is that 'Rudi' is a dead ringer for Björn Andrésen, the Swedish teenager who plays Dirk Bogarde's unrequited lust interest in the new film *Death in Venice*, the one *Jackie* call *'the world's most beautiful boy'*. On the dollies' gorgeousometer, 'Rudi' scores a perfect ten.

'Being in a group appeals to my ego,' Freddie twinkles. 'I love being the centre of attention. I like people to look at me when I'm walking down the road.'

The papers give Freddie all the attention he craves. He, in return, gives them the incredible truer than true life story of Rudi Valentino, né Frederick Burrett. Born in London, he grew up in a dreary town in Buckinghamshire. He went to a boys' school, which he didn't like since he much preferred playing with girls and making clothes for his cousin's dolls. He was taught to sew by his mum when he was 'oooh, knee-high' and by 15 was designing ladies' coats for Aquascutum. Nowadays he makes his own 'very expensive' one-off garments mainly for men, like David, such as a white tunic trimmed with emerald bands, worn with a pleated skirt.

'Designing and making clothes is my life much more than singing ever could be,' he admits. 'David thought my style of dress and appearance was great and he was looking for someone original. I must admit I'm not a very good singer, but I don't suppose that really matters.'

Let loose in print, Freddie is ten years of inhibitions ahead of his time. 'I look gay,' he tells *Sounds*, 'I suppose it's pretty obvious.' A pop star much too new and romantic for airwaves that can just about handle Indiana wanting R. Dean Taylor for *murder*, OK, but nothing *depraved*.

David, regardless, predicts the Arnold Corns will somehow succeed by 'copying the Stones', who everyone knows, 'and The Stooges', who everyone doesn't. He fulfils the first half of his pledge with a new song especially for Freddie called 'Looking For A Friend', a bit like 'Brown Sugar' if written not by Jagger/Richard but Julian/Sandy. This time, Freddie gets as far as the studio microphone to pucker a few breathy asides – *'oh so nice!'* – rendering its hopes of getting released even slimmer than a song glorifying cruising ever could be. Gigs are suggested, though the fact that the Arnold Corns never grace a concert stage brings Freddie no end of relief. 'I don't want to go on anywhere rough,' he fusses, 'I don't think I could cope. I mean, if they put us on at some of those places out of London, I'd get sent up something rotten by all those butch provincial blokes.' Better that they make music for the discotheque. Or, as Freddie euphemistically nudges, *'specialised* clubs'.

With all effort invested in the carry-on of camping, the record itself, 'Moonage Daydream', is lost. David's estimation of its uniqueness fails to echo among the few critics prepared to indulge its pretence.

'Rudi double-tracks frenziedly while the trio pounds away with little imagination,' boos *Disc*.

'It's a somewhat overforced bit of work,' hisses *Record Mirror. 'Good try, but a miss.'*

For David, a freak-out misfired, but not wasted, nor its flipside, 'Hang On To Yourself'. The right songs, just the wrong band at the wrong time playing in the wrong make-up. Instructive mistakes easily corrected. Just as soon as he finds the right space face.

ELEVEN

NOBODY IS QUITE WHO THEY SEEM ANYMORE. Monday nights on BBC Two, young British hearts gallop to the rowdy old west and a new *Butch Cassidy & The Sundance Kid*. Except Butch and Sundance are Hannibal Heyes and Kid Curry. Except Heyes and Curry are *Alias Smith and Jones*. Except Smith and Jones are Hollywood actors Pete Duel and Ben Murphy. The dolly mags blush over Murphy's doppelgängbang of Paul Newman and Ryan O'Neal, but it's the swarthy Duel, with his tragic-handsome smile like a Jimmy Webb ballad scored in brown eyes and dimples, whose face papers more bedroom walls. 'Working is a relief to me,' Duel tells the press. 'I can forget the troubles of the world and create something else – right now with *Alias*, it's a light-hearted, fun sort of world.' Except the real Duel is a heavy-hearted, serious sort of depressive who lists his hobbies as 'life and truth', haunted by a recent drunk-driving charge that cost him his licence. A man tormented by the show's rushed production, scrappy scripts and the repetition of always playing the same character. 'The ultimate trap,' he'll confide, 'you slowly lose any artistic thing you may have. It's utterly destructive.' And how. Before 1971 has chimed its final bell, the 31-year-old body of Pete Duel will be found lying in front of the Christmas tree in his Hollywood home beside the .38 calibre revolver he used to blow a hole through his right temple, hours after watching a fatally unsatisfying episode of *Alias Smith and Jones*.

On screen, off screen, it's all a performance.

'Ladies and gentlemen . . . MR ELVIS PRESLEY!'

The best-kept secret in the history of live entertainment is wasted on a parkful of potheads waiting to hear Pink Floyd play 'Alan's Psychedelic Breakfast'. Wild rumours have been circulating all day that The King is going to be the surprise guest at the Crystal Palace Garden Party and – *unbelievably* – here he is! The oily quiff, the yodelling hips, the blue suede shoes and gold lamé jacket . . . but why does the Elvis of 1971 look like the Elvis of 1956? And why is the jacket not actually lamé but velvet? And why, beneath that quiff, does the most beautiful man who ever lived now resemble a steelworker from Scunthorpe called Malcolm?

Because 'Elvis' *is* a steelworker from Scunthorpe called Malcolm. Or as he prefers 'Raving Rupert'. On the stage of the Palace Bowl, Rupert raves through 'Hound Dog', and those too stoned to tell the difference will wake up tomorrow with the haziest half-memory of a yesterday ruined by rain, beer queues, Floyd's giant inflatable octopus that didn't inflate and a stinking turn by *the* Elvis Presley.

Fake kings, fake queens, it's all a performance.

'I suppose you could call me the Danny La Rue of rock,' says the man born Vincent who calls himself Alice Cooper: underdressed, oversexed and over here hoping to export his Halloween schlock-rock. *'He knocks out the young boys with the daring of his act and rebelliousness of his image,'* reckons *Life* magazine. *'After all, the ultimate rebellion of our time is the simple refusal to be a man.'* The mascara-blinded Alice refuses to be a man by refusing to deny he once bit the head off a live chicken on stage, declaring 'women should be used as sex objects' and singing Rolf Harris songs with a band the *NME* liken to *'a freaky bunch of faggy pooves'*. Alice agrees. 'We come on like amphetamine drag queens.' All of it all too hilarious for the gossip page of *Record Mirror*.

'ALICE COOPER himself in London this week – if he bumps into DAVID BOWIE could be some tiffs over dress sense.'

Faggy or draggy, it's all a performance.

But still no joke over at the BBC. Not up in the gallery of Studio 3 as Tony Blackburn introduces this week's number 20 from Peter Noone. Not as a producer double-takes at the monitors and realises what he sees behind Herman singing about pretty things – is that a *male* Lauren Bacall playing piano?

'How the hell did *that pervert* get on *Top of the Pops*?'

DEFRIES AWAKES! His nightmare is over. The one that begins in the first thaw of January when a well-dressed gentleman from Minneapolis walks into the offices of Gem above Regent Street, introducing himself as Mr Don Hunter – songwriter, producer and business manager of a million-selling multi-instrumental wunderkind whose contract with Motown records is set to expire on his approaching 21st birthday. The nightmare of believing that he, Tony Defries – this time last year still a legal clerk with Messrs Godfrey, Davis & Batt – now has the opportunity to manage Stevie Wonder.

Laurence believes it too. Hunter brings Stevie in to meet them, the blind genius greeting his new friends by gently tapping the contours of their faces. Laurence's moustache, he tickles. Defries's afro, he loves. They sit with Hunter and discuss Stevie's predicament. He's been one of Motown's biggest consistent successes since the age of 12 – eleven Top 10 hits in America, five in the UK – but, now older and wiser, he's lost faith in label boss Berry Gordy. Marvin Gaye had the same problems but the emotional advantage of being Gordy's son-in-law, a stand-off he's just won with the belated release of *What's Going On*. Stevie isn't so lucky, his own albums still held to account by Gordy's traditional restraints. But that all ends on 13 May 1971. Stevie's contract is up, and if Gordy can't agree a new deal granting full creative control, he's free to sign with a new management and new label who will. This is Hunter's bait. Defries and Laurence gobble it up. And so the blind lead the blind.

Stevie celebrates his 21st birthday with a party in Detroit. Gordy is there. Most of Motown are there. Defries and Laurence are not.

Both men are over 500 miles away fretting in a Minneapolis hotel room, still waiting for the phone call from Stevie's lawyer confirming his signature on their new management contract. It doesn't come.

Panic takes its grip. They start ringing different numbers trying to speak to Stevie. No one will answer.

Finally, Laurence gets hold of Stevie's wife, Syreeta. 'I can't talk about it,' she says. Then hangs up.

The men from Gem have been in America over a week ironing out the deal. It meant Laurence missing his sacred Arsenal beating Liverpool in the FA Cup final, winning the double for the first time in their history – as he'd prayed – a noble sacrifice that would have been worth it. *Would* have.

Laurence places the receiver back on its cradle. He turns to Defries. Instinct tells him. 'It's over.'

Defries is silent. The same silence after a very tall building's been demolished by a controlled explosion. The specific annihilated silence of dreams turned to dust. Dreams so cocksure, he even told *Billboard* magazine in advance. *'Tony Defries flew to the US last week to complete the deal with Wonder to administer his activities throughout the world.'* Now a $1.25 newsstand laughing stock, in black and white.

There is no deal. In the end, Stevie re-signs with Motown: Gordy offers him a new contract, a better one allowing him to make the music he wants. And – oh, look! – there's Stevie in the charts now with his new single. A Beatles cover. 'We Can Work It Out.'

A fly buzzing in a Minneapolis hotel room hears an English voice scream.

'I HOPE THE BASTARD GOES FUCKING DEAF!'

So the nightmare ends, and Defries awakes. And in the groggy rush of reality returning, hears the distant tinkle of a familiar forgotten hope.

'Oh, you pretty things . . .'

And remembers. He owns this.

For the first time since signing with Defries over a year ago, David Bowie has a hit. Not *his* hit, but his song. 'Oh! You Pretty Things', the solo debut single by the Hermit formerly known as Herman, now plain Peter Noone, enters the charts at 34. The following week it leapfrogs 'Good Old Arsenal' by the victorious Arsenal 1st Team Squad to number 20. By the middle of June, it's number 12. Which means David has it in him to be a success after all. Though none of this was Defries's doing.

Ever since the carrot of signing, sealing and delivering Stevie dangled above his lap, Defries stopped worrying about what he ought to be doing with David, who fell from his thoughts quicker than Arsenal's Bob McNab brought down Liverpool's Steve Heighway in the sixth minute of extra time. In the interim, with his management lost in Wonderland,

David has been left to his own dangerously eccentric devices: inviting the tabloids to his house to photograph him in one of his dresses, scheming deals with his publisher, Bob, to put out the Arnold Corns single, and landing arm in arm with Freddie on the cover of a top-shelf sex magazine called *Curious*. But now Defries has woken, that all stops.

David has written a hit. The next one will be his own, of this Defries is certain. David is going to be a superstar – *his* superstar – just like he told him and Angie last year. 'You are the beginning, potentially, of an empire.' Defries meant it, every word.

Only he didn't promise that David would necessarily be its emperor.

A GIFT FOR THE NEW CAESAR. Personally delivered by David to the Regent Street offices of Gem in the first hayfevered sneeze of summer. A prize trophy of flesh and blood, but it's purely the flesh which makes Defries's eyes pop like bubble gum, in the same instant deafened by the quake of kettle drums walloping inside his skull like the theme from *2001: A Space Odyssey*. For if music be the food of love, such is the sonic boom of Dana Gillespie.

She is 21 with long dark hair and dark gypsy eyes, wise – if wary – with the understanding that her face is not the physical attribute people first notice. Not until, like Defries, they recover from the initial awe of her magnificent tits.

Everyone loves Dana's tits. David loves her tits. Angie loves her tits. Their friends down the Sombrero, some of whom have never met Dana because she doesn't go there, love her tits purely because whenever David and Angie talk about their friend Dana they rave about the size of her fantastic tits. They are . . . *fantastic*. Whoppers. Corkers. Bobbydazzling belters. Taj Mahals. The eighth and ninth wonders of the natural world. Geometrical marvels the great Renaissance master Brunelleschi would have applauded as in every measurement the equals of his dome of Florence Cathedral. Dana's is a bosom that would cushion the blow of any man throwing himself off the nearest roof trying to get a better look – and few wouldn't risk a 20-storey dive to get close to such phwoar-roaring, pint-spilling, fag-dropping, knee-buckling, glasses-steaming, eyes-crossing, horn-honking, seal-oinking, wolf-panting, traffic-stopping, car-crashing, ladder-toppling, cannon-firing, bouncing-bombing, reason-robbing, melon-trucking, Bristol-citying, knock-knockering, milk-jugging, bazooka-joeing, jelly-wobbling, bap-buttering, clang-clanging, ding-dinging, zing-zinging, luvverly-buncha-coconuting, sing-hosanna tits.

But her tits are not the reason David's brought her to Defries. Dana is a singer-songwriter, same as him. 'She could be a female Elton John,' says David. 'The trouble is that nobody's bothered to really take much interest in her.' Which, from the neck upwards, is sadly true.

She was born Richenda Antoinette de Winterstein Gillespie, her bloodline a state banquet of Sirs, Captains, Colonels, Lieutenant Commanders and similar decorated Henrys and Charleses. Dana is by birth a toff, Kensington-raised and Chelsea-schooled, but a markedly bohemian toff whose parents occupy separate floors of the same SW7 townhouse with their respective lovers, allowing their daughter to do as she pleases in its basement flat where, aged 15, she did as she pleased by sleeping with 17-year-old David.

The Gillespies are a thoroughly modern family.

Dana calls her flat 'the Bunker', although its ceiling has witnessed so much sex it could probably do with changing a vowel. Furnished with rugs and wall hangings like a Turkish bazaar, the Bunker is where the celluloid fantasy of Jagger's pad in *Performance* ends and libertarian reality begins. David still visits the Bunker – with Angie – and sometimes still sleeps with Dana – with Angie. There is plenty of Dana to go around, and David and Angie do so till they're giddy.

The Bowies are a thoroughly modern couple.

As a singer, Dana's only problem, as David explains to Defries, is one of image. When signed to Pye in the mid-Sixties, aged 16, she was first marketed as a Marianne Faithfull clone wailing a dismal Yiddish folk song about animal slaughter. Switching to Decca, she then became a ready steady mod chick purring a groovy Donovan tune. Neither Dana took off. Keeping her options open, Dana has since tried acting, last seen in a fantasy Hammer horror film about killer seaweed, giant crabs and the Spanish Inquisition. In the wardrobe equivalent of sending coals to Newcastle, she makes her screen entrance tied to a couple of barrage balloons. As Dana suspects, being Hammer they only wanted her 'for my tits'.

This, proposes David, is where Defries can help. The last time her name made the papers was a few months ago when she replaced P.P. Arnold as Bianca in the cast of the rock'n'roll *Othello* musical *Catch My Soul* at the Roundhouse. They never said anything about her singing, just ran a photo of her in her revealing stage costume so male readers could get an extra tuppence worth of tits. 'She's a fantastic singer,' swears David. 'Her own writing has really improved over the last year.'

Across the desk, Dana smiles her smouldering gypsy smile. Defries's spine chimes like a tuning fork. 'OK,' he says softly, the frizz in his afro threatening to uncurl.

He stretches over a hand. Dana shakes it, skin touching skin. The freshly lit cigar in his mouth pivots stiffly to attention.

'Let me take care' – he smiles – 'of *everything*.'

TWELVE

THE DAYS GROW BRIGHTER, but for Angie heavier. Nine months and fit to drop. For David's sake she has no time to waste – he the kite glittering high in the sky, she the wind keeping him up there. Sickness, backache and fatigue like the sleeping death will not stop her. Living with Angie, says David, is like living with a blowtorch: it'll take more than swollen ankles to dampen her flame. She eats for two and thinks for three, a one-woman hydra of manager, stylist and mother-to-be. Stomach heaving, cheeks blowing and arms octopussing, teeth grimacing, full volume and no brakes. Phone calls to make, meetings to sort, money to chase, shopping to buy, baby clothes to sew. Ring, ring, ring! Plan, plan, plan! Stitch, stitch, stitch! Burn, burn, burn! As fast and bright as she can to keep her brain so busy it forgets how petrified she is that there's this *thing* bulging inside her ready to rip her in half any day now.

Any . . .

Call, call, call!

. . . day . . .

Go, go, go!

. . . NOW!

'SWEET JEEZUS!'

So it begins, in sodden legs, pink mucus and the first white-knuckle cramp. David drives Angie the two-mile panic to the hospital where she is trolleyed off to the maternity annexe. Passing half-open doorways and

80

unshut curtains she glimpses the faces of her cursed sisterhood. Waxy, pale, ready for embalming, refugees from Géricault's *The Raft of the Medusa* washed up and left for dead on the lonely shores of Bromley & District Hospital. The nearby sound of a baby wailing becomes the rasping hiss of a vulture circling overhead. Angie grimaces her best Angie-can-do-anything face. But Angie is afraid.

David does not loiter longer than necessary. The father of 1971 isn't expected to. *You go home, mister. Watch* Grandstand, *nip to the pub, have a pint, smoke some fags, grab a pie and chips and a good night's kip until the eventual phone call telling you if it's a boy or a girl and whether your missus survived the journey to hell and back. You've already done your bit, aintcha? Anyway, you can't help her now, mate, even if you wanted to. Nobody can.*

No, nobody can. Angie is entirely at the mercy of Kentish midwifery. There she lies, on her back, hair stuck to her clammy forehead, the bangles David placed on her wrist on their wedding day jingling madly as she squeezes her hands into fists so tight her fingernails cut into the palms. Surrounded by aproned strangers wincing at her screams as they mop her brow and tell her to keep pushing.

So, she pushes. *MARYMOTHEROFCUNTINGCHRIST!* She knows it's going to hurt, but there's hurt and hurt. *And this is fucking unreal!* Like she can't breathe because there's some motherfucker squeezing her stomach like she's trapped in an old whalebone corset, and they're yanking the laces, pulling it tighter and tighter and tighter, like they want to garotte her. And it goes on and on, forever, and fucking ever, like she wants to shit or vomit herself inside out, but she can't because all she's trying to do is breathe, like a salmon gasping on the riverbank begging to be thrown back in the water. On and on. Hours and hours. Until time stops, because there is no time, because it's never going to stop. Just like that Greek horror story about Prometheus chained to a rock and the eagle of Zeus flying down every day to peck out his liver while he's still alive because it's the worst pain the gods could conjure. And even worse, they curse him so the liver magically grows back every time to be pecked out again the next day, and so it goes on for all agonising eternity. *And it's the FUCKING SAME!* Only the rock is the bed, and the liver is her stomach that's going to explode, and the eagle is every fucking nurse and doctor yelling 'PUSH!' and 'BREATHE!' when there is never enough gas and air to stop the pain that's like a barbed-wire walrus headbutting her insides. She begs for the epidural. *PLEEEASE!* A big fat needle stabbing the spine like those mobsters in the movies sticking it in the back with an ice pick. *FUCKITHURTS!* So now she can't feel her legs and her head's floating like she's stoned. Bad stoned. And still it drags. Hours and hours, suffering and suffering, weaker and weaker, writhing clammy white flesh and tortured orifice against a canvas of plague black and offal purple and abattoir red like a painting by Francis Bacon. Until suddenly death feels very real and God must be either deaf or some seriously sick Gestapo bastard not to intervene. *HOLYFUCKINGJEEEEZUS! Do it to David! Do it to David! Not me! David! I don't care what you do to him. Tear his face off, strip his bones. Not me! David! Not me! ARRUGHAFUCKERRRRRRRRRRRRRRRRRRRRRRRRRRR!*

A pelvis cracks and a child is born. A boy, eight pounds, eight ounces. Angie's 30-hour labour is over.

In the drowsy Sunday morning yawn of Haddon Hall, David smokes a cigarette, the gentle whinny of Neil Young's *After The Goldrush* on the front-room stereo. A telephone shatters its sleepy rhythm. David answers and a nurse's voice informs him he is father to a son. The baby is fine, and the mother is resting. He thanks them and hangs up. A father.

'I believe in you,' sings Neil. The *'I'* becomes *'we'* when David sings as he strums his guitar, fingering a light melody around a D chord: the *'we'*, him and Angie, the *'you'* their baby boy. He keeps singing and strumming, nursery-rhyming about their lovers' story and how if their son is anything like them then he's going to grow up bananas. Sentimental slosh, he knows, but such a pretty tune he can't resist. He calls it 'Kooks'.

David drives to the hospital that afternoon. Angie has slept, but her face retains the terrible truth of someone whose skeleton has just been broken. She smiles weakly, they embrace, and David starts to cry. He wants to see their son. Angie tells him to go along to the nursery where he's being monitored with the other newborns. A nurse leads him along the corridor to a small room with rows of white cribs. David takes one look and his heart bursts. The soft little face, the tiny, tiny fingers. The mouth, just like Angie's, and the shape of the eyes just like his. He leans closer to touch. *We believe in you . . .*

'No, no,' says the nurse. 'That's not yours. The one next to it.'

David stops, straightens up and turns to the adjacent cot. Ah, yes! The soft little face, the tiny, tiny, fingers. Just like Angie, and just like him. *Oh, we believe in YOU!* Tears brim in his eyes as his shoulders shake with soft laughter.

Oh! Can you imagine? There he was, cooing over a baby Doug Yule – ha! – thinking it was a little Lou Reed.

THEY NAME HIM ZOWIE. Like Zoe – Greek for 'life' – to rhyme with Bowie. Even though most people read Zowie as 'Zow-ee', the way Joe E. Brown says it in *Some Like It Hot*, or like the *Batman* fight captions, or the prog compilation LP Decca put out last year, *Wowie Zowie*. David says he would rather they let the name evolve over time around the personality, but they have to call him something and so Zowie it is, if only as a gift to magazine subeditors.

'ZOWIE! IT'S THE BOWIES!'

For the time being, at least.

HE'D BEEN DRIVING up the M1 on his way to a ferry to Ireland when he heard the news on the radio. Overcome, he was forced to pull over on the hard shoulder where he sat alone in his car, sobbing tears of joy, and vindication. All the years he'd believed when the world laughed in his face, and now this fairy-tale ending. His friend had done it, just like they both always said he would. Marc Bolan was number 1.

But that was months ago, and DJ John Peel hasn't seen much of Marc since. When *Melody Maker* probe him on the current state of pop in '71, Peel is glibly pessimistic. 'We're going through a very sterile period,' he muses, T. Rex very far from his thoughts. 'People are basically more hung up on images than they are on music. They'd much rather go and see somebody famous than hear somebody good. You see, you get a situation where a Beatles or a Stones or an Elvis Presley are both good and glamorous but there isn't anybody who's both that at the moment, or both on that scale.'

Good, but not yet fully glamorous, David hopes to change Peel's mind tonight on stage at the BBC's Paris Theatre. It is the first week of June and his first concert of the year is to be pre-recorded live for broadcast on Radio

1's *Sounds of the 70s*. His backing band have been together barely 24 hours, with Woody and Trevor joining Mick in Haddon Hall only yesterday for a make-or-break rehearsal alongside Mark as extra rhythm guitarist. To complicate matters, David has also decided to invite his friends Dana, Geoff and George and let them each sing a song. As he plans it, it'll be a radio showcase for the vast ensemble of David Bowie Productions. Or, as Peel introduces, 'the music of David Bowie and a galaxy of his friends.'

It is a peculiar concert, David sometimes singing, sometimes not, and even when he does sing not always as himself. On his latest song about the Sombrero, 'Queen Bitch', he impersonates Lou Reed. On 'Bombers', he's Neil Young. On his Freddie cruising song, 'Looking For A Friend', he's Mick Jagger. Even his friends don't all sing like themselves. George sings David's 'Song For Bob Dylan', as required, in the style of Bob Dylan. Dana sings David's 'Andy Warhol' in the style of Grace Slick with a posh pinch of Honor Blackman. And Geoff sings backing on a Chuck Berry cover, 'Almost Grown', like a one-man Harvey & The Moonglows. All four singers unite, not that harmoniously, on 'It Ain't Easy', a greasy holy roller David picked up in America from Three Dog Night which sounds like something horrible Ian Gillan would rasp in *Jesus Christ Superstar*. The only time tonight David properly sounds like himself is when he debuts his new song of fatherhood, 'Kooks' – just his voice, his 12-string guitar, his honesty, his optimism, his love. It's the best performance of the night and he isn't even really *performing*.

Peel is unmoved to no tears but compliments David often between songs. For Mick it's all a fine excuse to Jeff'n'Jimi wherever the tune allows, while for Woody and Trevor it's a chance to earn their permanent mattresses up on the landing of Haddon Hall. After tonight, they do.

The audience, too, are as appreciative as any band could wish considering they've already had to sit through half an hour of patch-denimed folk rock from a group called Heron. It is only David who, afterwards, broods doubtfully. Perhaps he tried a little *too* hard to show off just what he's capable of? Not a pop singer, more a rock'n'roll variety turn. The man of a thousand voices – even Herman's as he reminds with a wonky bash through 'Oh! You Pretty Things' – still unsure for now which of them, if any, suits him the best. Time running wild, he'll have to decide. Maybe all. Maybe none. Maybe a new, starrier voice altogether.

Past midnight, and the theatre has emptied. David and the band have packed up and driven home to Beckenham. The crowd have long dispersed and outside on Lower Regent Street the pavements are a film noir waiting for a gunshot to ricochet from the shadows. Peel wanders alone towards the nearest tube station taking him back to Notting Hill, to the home he shares with his girlfriend, affectionately 'The Pig', and the two pet hamsters given to him by an old friend he sadly doesn't see much these days. While somewhere back in those concrete shadows, a head with no room for yesterdays shakes its black curls over a studio mixing desk, listening to the magic it's just pulled out of humbucker pickups and a notebook of poems it was thinking of calling 'Metal Mythology', now as renamed for the B-side of 'Get It On', 'Raw Ramp'. A sound as good as its creator is glamorous.

THIRTEEN

THE COSMOS IS CALLING. The ley lines say it. The new moon says it. The surrounding hills forming the 12 signs of the Zodiac say it. The nearby tor of Arthurian legend says it. The blind spring in the field where they're going to build the stage says it. The favourite book of T. Rex hunk Mickey Finn, *The View Over Atlantis* by John Michell, says it, and so do the organisers who've read and believed its megalithic lunacy including the granddaughter of Sir Winston Churchill. More urgently, the calendar says it. June 21. Summer Solstice.

Last year, when T. Rex were here, the planners had got it all wrong. They turned a Somerset dairy farm into a rock festival in the middle of September. The milk was free, but the vibes were off. But now the cosmos is calling – *'Midsummer!'* shout the stars, *'Midsummer!'* – and the Pilton prophets are listening. No more no-shows from the Kinks at the 'Worthy Farm Pop, Folk & Blues Festival'. This year the spaceship will land at 'Glastonbury Fair'.

Cosmic oracle-in-chief is Andrew Kerr, a 37-year-old public school dropout who looks like Rasputin and speaks like the BBC World Service. 'I got the idea that at a very special time – Summer Solstice – people got together to trap the fusion of the sun and many other things and drew down the astrological energies to stimulate life force to grow plants, to strengthen and fertilise the soil and the people.' Glastonbury Fair, he insists, is not just another rock festival but an opportunity to 'tap the universe'. The central faucet being the new stage designed in the shape of a 48-foot-high pyramid, constructed with to-the-inch perfection on the intersection of ley lines – as located by dowsing – its sides slanting at an exact angle of 51.43 degrees intended to sluice as much fertilising celestial fire from the heavens as is geometrically possible. The ground is sacred, they know, because of the vibrations, older than time, which have absolutely nothing to do with the electric pylons channelling 400,000 volts buzzing overhead. And unlike last year's Isle of Wight Festival – which was all about making bread, *man* – Glastonbury Fair is going to be free. Completely free.

Except for car parking because there isn't any. 'We've no room for cars,' says Kerr. And make sure you bring as much of your own food as possible, because there isn't any. And water, because there isn't any supply. And toilet paper, because there isn't any on site, and for that matter no toilets either, just one big trench being frantically dug deeper as the festival approaches to accommodate an estimated 8,000 hippies' worth of cidery piss and lentily shit. 'People must get it into their heads to live in complete wilderness for four days. If they're just going to trip down here to listen to music, it could be a terrible scene.'

A terrible scene with no posters, no tickets and no advertising. Just a sign on the main gate which reads:

> **You enter at your own risk – we cannot accept responsibility for ANYTHING that happens to you while you are on WORTHY FARM**

And still they trip down from every point on the compass, pilgrims of cerebral oblivion, heeding the spiral-eyed word from the nearest roach-sucking mouth. *'Glastonbury Fair!'* Hippies, heads, students, gyppos, bikers, pushers, cordwanglers, Hare Krishnas, Jesus freaks, Buddhists, Sufis, Bahá'ís, witches, druids and every crystal-swinging crackpot from Carlisle to Camden, here for spiritual enlightenment, cosmic vibrations, satori, abduction by aliens, the Second Coming, the age of Aquarius, free love, good dope, bad acid, blowbacks, blowjobs, nudity, mud baths, VD and the promise that at some point over the weekend at the very least Hawkwind and the Pink Fairies might lay down some heavy grooves. 'I happily don't know who's going to play,' boasts Kerr a week before the gate swings open. 'I'm doing this because I dig music as a form of spiritual expression.'

The main spiritual expressionists include Melanie, Terry Reid, the Edgar Broughton Band, Brinsley Schwarz and Arthur Brown, all of whose appearances up on the pyramid have been timed according to intricate astrological calculations: respectively, Aquarius, Scorpio, a mix of Scorpio, Taurus and Gemini, mainly Aries, and Cancer. A divine plan abruptly cocked up by the non-cosmic voodoo of British weather and occasional power failure. By day three, the zodiac is in disarray, much like the looted market stalls that popped up trying to flog joss sticks and incense. So when that evening's 7.30 p.m. slot predesignated for a specific Capricorn rolls around, things are badly overrunning. The heavens keep turning. The goat must wait.

DAVID, THE GOAT, retires to the comfort of the Eavis family farmhouse where he stays up until the early hours chatting with fellow musicians, drinking barley wine and smoking tincture of cannabis as his own planetary pull dictates. He's here with Angie, having entrusted Zowie to the care of Sue in Haddon Hall, hoping the festival vibes will help her somehow to recover the old Angie missing in action since her wiped-out return from the hospital. Mick is also here, for musical support, and Dana, for moral support, and Defries, ostensibly for David but more intimately for Dana, now receiving his deepest managerial attention.

Up on the silvery pyramid, the wailing, warbling, noodling and fiddling drags on into the indigo night. In the farmhouse, David waits up to see the first watery blue greys of dawn, the time when time has lost all meaning and neither yesterday nor tomorrow can decide which is today. He is past caring when the hour hand yawns that it's nearly 5 a.m. and he hears his name called. At last, the pyramid wants him. He rises from his soft seat, sparkly-eyed and fuzzy-headed, stage-ready in his Freddie-made loose cotton jacket and high-waist Oxford bags, offset with a pair of semi-wedge heels. He collects the blue cloak Angie made especially for him and tosses it around his shoulders, then a wide-brimmed embroidered felt hat which he pushes down over his flowing hair. He is resplendent. He is stoned. He is ready.

The audience isn't. The largest David's ever faced is half-asleep and half-alive. Brains soft-boiled by dope, trepanned by acid or blinded by scrumpy. From the stage it's like looking at an army camp after a battle. Tents as far as he can see all the way to the trees, scattered bodies, spreadeagled and lifeless, heads lolling, pupils rolled so far back in their heads their eyes seem pure zombified white, huddled together under blankets, wandering aimlessly, gazing up at him in blank expectation. *Do something, o holy man, in your wizard's cloak and funny hat.*

He has only his 12-string guitar, his Woolworths organ and whatever electric ballast Mick chooses to pile on top. In the chilly dew of dawn his fingers stiffen and for the first couple of songs he frets clumsily. Mick's hands are no warmer and in the cold air the speakers crackle like a sickly cough. It does not sound good.

David switches to his electric organ and sparks up a ready-rolled. He is about to play when he sees a beetle crawling over the keyboard. 'There's a beetle on my keyboard,' he tells the crowd and several heads nod with profound cosmic understanding. Rather than try and flick it off he starts playing around it, stretching his fingers to stab whatever weird chords he can find that spare him squishing innocent insect life. He giggles, stoned. So do those gathered near the base of the pyramid. The beetle flies away. David laughs and starts telling a story about a song he wrote called 'I'd Like A Big Girl With A Couple of Melons'. He sings one verse before he's suddenly interrupted on stage by a big girl with a couple of melons. Such is the wish-come-true astrological energy of the Glastonbury pyramid.

'She's here!' cries David.

Big Melons plonks herself on the stool beside him. He asks where she's from and she tells him Sweden. He would ask if she's off her gourd, but her eyes already tell him twice as much as he is. He begins to play 'Oh! You Pretty Things' and by the first chorus Big Melons is joining in. Her singing is awful. David starts to crack up.

'This is about homo superior, love, you're letting the lyrics down badly.'

She stays where she is, moaning and giggling, tripping and flopping until David manages to gently nudge her away.

'Go get some bacon and eggs!'

Chuckles ricochet in the crowd. Big Melons staggers to the rear of the stage and mercifully topples out of sight.

There are more attentive bodies now. Squint-eyed heads poking through tent flaps to see what all the meloning and mama-papa-ing is about. A first ray of morning sun slices through the clouds as he switches back to guitar for 'Kooks'. Its sweet melody acts like an inverse lullaby, rocking Worthy Farm awake. People aren't just listening – they're *really* listening, bopping heads, swaying and smiling, not all of it the last shivers of wine and resin. Whatever universe they came here to find, David is tapping into it. He is moved to thank them.

'I just want to say that you've given me more pleasure than I've had in a good few months . . .'

Claps and cheers.

'. . . I don't do gigs anymore because I got so pissed off with dying a death every time. It's really nice to have somebody appreciate me for a change.'

The cheers grow louder. Back at his organ, David fingers the opening notes of 'Memory Of A Free Festival', the song he wrote nearly two years ago about the festival he and his friends organised in Beckenham, the one he didn't enjoy though the song made out he had, almost as much as he's enjoying this one. And so he sings it, like he was always meant to sing it, here in its perfect moment, sitting on the great pyramid surveying several thousand children of the stars, ley lines throbbing under his feet. And as he sings, the sunlight begins to burn away the clouds, brighter and brighter, until he's reached the song's 'Hey Jude' climax, praising be the coming of the sun machine. And as he repeats the chorus, over and over, the pyramid illuminates, its metallic surface glowing with the bouncing reflections of the midsummer dawn. And as the pyramid sparkles, the crowd join in, chanting about sun machines and partying, *uh-huh-huh*. And as the crowd sings, the naked sun whips its rays across the sky in pinks and golds, its centre approaching-spaceship bright, looking like it might actually be about to land in the middle of a field two miles southwest of Shepton Mallet. The Solstice passed, later than billed, Glastonbury Fair finally welcomes its true cosmic messiah.

And then David ruins it by singing his depressing Jacques Brel song about Amsterdam. He says goodbye, then floats off into the morning. Leaving Glastonbury to finish waking up before puffing onwards to its final skullfucked night.

THIS TIME NEXT WEEK the field will be full of cows again and the cafés in the village will have removed their temporary signs in the window reading 'NO HIPPIES'.

The hippies will be too busy passing judgement in the underground press, some calling Glastonbury *'a freaks' Butlins'*, others *'more about dope and good times than cosmic-oneness – a good case of brain damage was enjoyed by all'*.

Kerr and the organisers will be five grand in debt, desperately thinking of ways to make up the deficit.

The pyramid stage will be dismantled and will remain so since Glastonbury Fair will not happen again for another eight years.

The pylons will still buzz 400,000 volts overhead and a nauseating smell of rotten shite will hang heavy over the filled-in toilet trench for weeks.

Jimmy Savile will present that week's *Top of the Pops* wearing shorts with a smiley face sticker over his genitals, and for the second week running number 1 will be 'Chirpy Chirpy Cheep Cheep' by Middle Of The Road, a Glasgow group, formerly Los Caracas, led by a hairdresser called Sally, formerly Sarah.

The *NME* will ponder whether the *'New Pop Messiah?'* might be James Taylor, while Marc will have told yet another magazine his plans for a sci-fi film 'about a cosmic messiah'.

Every pop critic will agree that the new T. Rex single, 'Get It On', is 'another instant number 1' and that *'Boly's done it again!'*

The Who will announce their own single, 'Won't Get Fooled Again', with press adverts featuring drummer Keith Moon dragged up in women's lingerie and a blonde wig.

And David will be home in Beckenham, leafing through that day's *Daily Mirror* with its new photo of his long hair, floppy hat, blouse and baggy slacks, beside Angie, with her short hair, wearing what she calls her furry 'lumberjack' coat and boots, pushing baby Zowie in his pram, and the headline – 'RIGHT THEN, WHICH ONE'S DAD?' On the opposite page, an advert for drills – *'If you don't take steps, things could get out of control in your household.'*

And way, way up above, the distant stars keep beaming their centuries-old light at our silly little planet, like so many million peals of ancient laughter.

FOURTEEN

ANGIE IS STILL MISSING. Her body is here, her voice, her face, sometimes even the ghost of her smile, but it's just the body. The spirit is gone, the blowtorch not blowing. She is a mother broken, a woman with 18 stinging stitches where no woman wants to be stitched, and, because of it, now a National Health junkie withdrawing from painkillers. As much as she loves her son, he frightens her. Zowie cries, and cries, and cries, and cries, and will not stop crying no matter how much she cuddles, rocks, kisses and whispers to him.

But it's not Zowie she really fears. It's herself. Her own uselessness, and guilt, that the baby clothes she made, the cot they painted, the toys they bought, none of it means two beans to her anymore. Motherhood isn't a joy but a never-ending test willing her to fail. Sterilising bottles and teats, changing nappies, baby burps and beddy-byes, all of it daring her to make one tiny mistake to remind her how disgracefully fucking hopeless a mommy she actually is. David does his coochy-cooing best, and she has the saviour Sue from downstairs as an extra pair of female arms. But then Zowie cries again, and Angie picks him up and gently rocks him. And he keeps crying and crying and crying, so much she begins to cry herself out of sheer exhaustion. Then passes him to Sue, and in three swings in Sue's bosom the crying stops. And just so she never forgets, there's David's mum, Peggy, with her knife-twisting tongue and salt-rubbing eyes every time she pops over to see her grandson. All over again, Angie feels like the worst mum in history.

No, Angie is missing. The fire, the force, the fabulousness. The screaming capital ANGIENESS. Like she accidentally flushed out her soul along with the placenta. Her GP reassures her that her symptoms are not uncommon. It has a name – post-partum depression – not that anyone in 1971 ever discusses it outside a doctor's surgery. Just part of the small print of pregnancy they never teach you in school, along with stillbirth, dying in labour and the scars like someone's been at your vulva with a tomahawk.

As the sleep-starved days drag by, Angie rapidly deteriorates. Everyone in Haddon Hall can see she's in trouble. David, Mick, Woody, Trevor, Sue downstairs and her boyfriend Tony, even Mark and his mum Donna over in Walnut Court. 'She's not the same bubbly Angie, is she?' And none of them has any clue how to bring her bubbles back. Except for Dana.

The Gillespies of Kensington being the sort of baronial family who own an Italian villa on the shore of Lake Maggiore, and Dana being the sort of friend who can't bear to see a gal in peril, she demands Angie join her there for a week of medicinal Alpine sun. David does not object. Sue, already their nanny in all but name, agrees to help him look after Zowie while Angie's away. It may even be a permanent solution. 'Children need a nanny,' Angie justifies, stuffing clothes into a suitcase, 'so they don't pick up their parents' neuroses.' David says nothing, quietly thinking of his dad, and of Peggy, and of Terry who their mum abandoned, and of how many neuroses it takes to end up in the Cane. Angie finishes packing. Outside, a taxi beeps. A goodbye kiss. 'I'll call.' And she is gone.

Leaving David holding the baby, gurgling oblivious, as a sadness slowly creeps up on him, like a bank of black cloud blocking out the sun over a summer festival. *You won't be sorry?* Oh, Zowie. So much for the lovers' story, stuck here with just the one kook. And the whole country will keep singing that bloody song on the radio.

Where's your mama gone? WHERE'S YOUR MAMA GONE?

★

WHERE THERE'S A MIDDLE OF THE ROAD, there's always a hard shoulder. In 1971 its name is Mott The Hoople: to the weekly inkies, the wildest thing on ten legs ever to have trembled a concert stage. Gig reviews read like scenes from the Sack of Rome: *'a gigantic raving party'*, inciting *'audience mayhem'* among *'a writhing mass of mesmerized rock children'*. The big mystery being why, after three years, Mott can't translate these riotous packed houses into record sales?

Maybe because their first album was too rushed, their second too depressing and their third too weedy. And because their original tunes aren't that memorable and their choice of covers, including the Sombrero last dance of Melanie's 'Lay Down', completely pointless. And because frontman Ian Hunter's idea of singing is roughly the same as his idea of hoarsely yelling to a mate across a crowded pub. In the provincial front-row crush, Mott are rock'n'roll personified: on the cold grooves of a turntable, rock'n'roll crucified. But Mott will not, and cannot, be stopped. Their label is so certain they splash out on a four-page advertorial in the *NME*: *'The time is right – the future secured – this then is the beginning.'* This, then, being the historic occasion of Mott The Hoople in the Royal Albert Hall.

'There are two schools of thought on rock music today,' says Hunter. 'One is exemplified by Emerson, Lake & Palmer who play completely technical music for the heads. Ours comes from the balls.'

Truly, the Albert Hall hasn't heard bollocks like it. The PA system pumps a greasy porridge of crashes, bangs and wallops while Hunter's throat scrapes notes as he might fag butts off the soles of his boots. Which is everything Mott's fans paid as much as £1.90 and as little as 30p for. Their new single, 'Midnight Lady', is introduced with the alarming 'news' that Tony Blackburn has promised to shoot himself if it makes the charts. The Visigoths' approving roar wakes Albert in his grave. Behind and above the band, the great pipe organ once tickled by Saint-Saëns gazes down in stiff dismay as the denimed *danse macabre* unfolds: box ceilings crack, bodies pile up onto the stage, heads threaten to shake off their shoulders and boots stamp like the beating shields of a Zulu army. When the houselights rise, pale ushers tot up the wreckage: 36 loggia boxes, three stall entrances, two chairs, one door, 12 curtain cords and poles and one gentlemen's lavatory tap. Total damages: £1,465 and 74 pence.

Nobody is particularly shocked when Mott are banned for life from the Albert Hall; reports of the vandalism even convince halls in Brighton and Cheltenham to twitchily cancel bookings. At least the BBC still allow them on *Top of the Pops* to play 'Midnight Lady' as a recommended new release, for all the difference it makes. The day after it airs, sales of the single strangely plummet. Mott don't make the charts and Tony Blackburn doesn't have to shoot himself. Not that the DJ *Honey* magazine bracket with Herman and Cliff as 'the man-next-door type' owns a gun – just an E-type Jag, a motorbike and a Regent's Park flat with six TV sets, a £500 video recorder so he can tape *The Dick Emery Show*, a reproduction of Constable's *Hay Wain* and a sparse kitchen for his weekly shopping list consisting of six tins of Batchelors peas, six tins of salmon, one carton of milk and a packet of biscuits. 'Because,' says Blackburn, 'I'm lonely a lot of the time.'

While Hunter, in his new flat off Wandsworth Common, with his shelves of history books on the American Civil War and biographies of Adolf Hitler – 'he interests me a lot' – licks his wounds, writing new songs about suicide, brooding aloud how they might be omens for the future of the most popular live band of no-hit losers in the land.

'I'm wondering just how long we can go on?'

DAVID HAS NOT BEEN DRIVING so much this summer. Not since the Riley accident. And, besides, as he once said himself over a midnight spliff, 'You never saw Garbo drive a car.' Better, where possible, not to drive but be driven. And better still, when the horse chestnuts are in full summer candelabra, to take a stroll, like Garbo, through Beckenham's Victorian landscaped park known locally as 'Bec Rec'.

He reaches the old bandstand, welded by Glasgow brawn, eroded by waxed moustaches, polished buttons and parping brass, momentarily lost in his sepia moment of two summers past. Community, love, happiness – and death. The summer of '69 when his father died, when David and his friends organised their free festival here. He'd stood on this very spot, singing 'Space Oddity' to a lawn of long hair, cheesecloth, paisley, denim and smoke, enjoying none of it, even though he'd write the song he sang at Glastonbury pretending he had. But that was then. Today is a new memory to make and a better song to sing. Then, like a prayer answered, it hits him.

Baa-baa, ba-da ba-da bap bap.

Out of nowhere. Out of the sky, out of flower beds, out of the night plume of a blackbird and the holy whisper of a yew. Beyond the sun, beyond the stars, beyond the spectrum of light.

Baa, baa . . .

A melody.

Ba-da . . .

And in another surge of neurons, a word.

'Sai-lors!'

Everything in the world stops turning except for the tune in David's head. It spins with him, out through the park gates, onwards up the high street, past the cinema advertising the new *Wuthering Heights*, to the bus-stop queue where everyone's thoughts are on time, traffic and decimal coinage except his, waltzing out of his body on cosmic rays, 90 million miles to the nearest planet out in space.

Ba-da ba-da bap bap!

Until, after a memory blank of stepping on the number 54 that his brain is too busy to record, he finds he is moving. No, the world is moving. The grubby window becomes his silver screen. Sad faces, fragile lives, little England, the George pub, the butchers, the bakers, the railway station. The Trumptonshire smallness of everything.

'Sai-lors!'

Where is everyone going? Where is *he* going?

Ba-da ba-da bap bap!

Lewisham. That's it. When he got up this morning he decided he might go to Lewisham to buy some new threads. Well, that was the plan.

'Sai-lors!'

But the sailors are pressganging him. They know it and he knows it. This one's from The Gods and if he stays on the bus their gift will be lost in the swish of a clothes rail. The tune booms louder and his heart quickens. The next stop on Southend Road is approaching. Home, his piano and the posterity of pencil and tape recorder are only minutes away. The cavemen rage and the sailors roar. Now or never: it's his choice.

Ba-da ba-da bap bap!
And suddenly, there is no choice . . .

AN HOUR LATER, in Lewisham, a pair of trousers is sold to somebody who won't look nearly so good in them as David, had he only been there to buy them first. While in Beckenham, a baby flaps its short, fat limbs as a piano goes *ba-da ba-da bap bap* and his daddy sings about sailors and cavemen, understanding none of it.

WHY, WHO'S THIS? Who is it, Zowie? It's Daddy! That's right. *Da-dee.* Isn't he funny? With his soft, hempy smell and his long hair and his ever-so-queer eyes, can you see them? See how that one looks blue and the other looks almost brown. And those daft white jaggedy things flashing in his mouth every time he smiles. Those are called teeth, Zowie. *Teeth.* You'll have yours soon – maybe they'll even grow as crazy as Daddy's! Wouldn't that be *hilarious*?

And what about this funny-looking fellow? This is your Uncle Trevor, and those furry things are called sideburns. *Side-burns.* But it'll be a while before your little chubby cheeks can grow a pair, Zowie – certainly not a pair as big as Uncle Trevor's! And this is Uncle Woody. He makes all that noise you hear echoing from the hall. *Bash, bash!* Remember? They're called drums. Woody plays the drums with Daddy, and Trevor plays a type of guitar called a bass, and then there's Uncle Mick. That's right, the one with the kind eyes and lashes like a cow. *Moo, moo!* Only this cow goes *twang, twang!* Mick plays a guitar too. He's very good at it. He also makes awful smells in the kitchen. Curried beans. He stinks the place out something awful, doesn't he? Silly smelly old Uncle Mick. But we still love him dearly, don't we, Zowie?

And, look, we've got a visitor. Another funny man with floppy blond hair and a happy face. This is Uncle Rick. What do we say, Zowie? *'Hello, Uncle Rick!'* Rick plays the piano and he's very, very good at it. He's popped over so Daddy can teach him some of his new songs. You might hear them practising later. How does the piano go again? *Plink, plonk!* That's it. Daddy's always plinking and plonking these days, isn't he?

And, oh, now, just look at all this loveliness all around you. Pink walls and red curtains and soft cushions and big rugs and shiny things and pictures everywhere. What's this one, Zowie? Those are fairies, like the ones living at the bottom of the garden. And who's in this picture? Daddy? No, but close. It's Greta Garbo. *Gar-bo.* And who are these? These are The Doors – see, 'D-O-O-R-S' and that says '*L.A. Woman*' and this is an LP Daddy borrowed off Uncle Mark who lives across the road. And that man there with the big beard is called Jim Morrison, only he's just died and we're all very sad about that, aren't we, Zowie? Poor, poor Jim! And what's this here? Why, it's Daddy's guitar, the one he plays when he sings you to sleep with that special kooky song he wrote just for you. And – oh, now, wait! Whose is *this* face that's just come through the door? It's not Lovely Sue from downstairs to give you another cuddle. And it's much too young a face to be your Granny Jones. But whoever's it is, it's a very happy face, isn't it? Rosy and glowing, like a freshly poked fire. Leaning in closer, and closer and . . . oh, Zowie, can you see now?

Mummy's home!

FIFTEEN

MERCURY ARE WINDED BY THE MESSENGER. 'David Bowie will never record another note for you.' The voice is Defries, the words straight from the *Allen Klein Book of Corporate Ballbreaking*.

David's contract with Mercury says otherwise: he still owes them a third album. 'You won't get it,' promises Defries. Lawyers flap and letters fly but his position remains firm. A begrudging Mercury budge enough to insist he buy David out of his deal to recoup their losses. A figure is agreed, but only after Defries wrangles the return of the rights for the two albums David's already given them – the one with 'Space Oddity' called *David Bowie*, and *The Man Who Sold The World*. Since neither have made them any money, Mercury gladly cash the settlement cheque in the short-sighted delusion of victory.

And so David is free. But, as of now, label-less.

Up in their Regent Street war cabinet of Gem Music, Defries and Laurence chew over a plan. They *could* take the obvious route and set up meetings with various interested parties to secure David a new recording contract. But Defries sees a better solution. The best way to guarantee a deal, in their favour, is to finance David's next album themselves, presenting it to prospective labels as a fait accompli: the first LP of a new contract, on their terms. This way David still belongs to Gem while the record company is a mere licensee. Laurence nods. 'I like it.' Just as well since as Gem's major shareholder he, not Defries, will be paying for it.

David is ecstatic. He's been ready to record for months. As far back as January he was telling the press he'd 'enough stuff to do another two albums'. That was before he had a band. Now he has, and the songs, and a restored confidence after the Herman hit and his reception at Glastonbury. He doesn't know it yet, but he also has the album cover from his most recent publicity shoot in May: wearing his and Angie's shared lumberjack coat, mannered hands sweeping the hair back from either side of his face exactly as Garbo used to do in her studio portraits for MGM. And, as Peel forewarned listeners to Radio 1's *Sounds of the 70s*, David already knows the album's title.

'*Hunky Dory*.'

THE FRUIT FLY HEAT OF JULY, the broken neon heart of Soho. A few feet beneath the tread of sad men's shoes stumbling to the nearest beaded doorway to rattle its jingling sucker alarm lies buried treasure. Trident Studios. Stardust still settling in the air like the scent of an animal marking its territory. The scent of Marc: it's his territory. He's just been here finishing the new T. Rex album, singing about Cadillacs, flying saucers and dancing himself out of the womb. Vibes that will do David no harm whatsoever: he, too, is here to be born again.

A new face at the mixing console. An easy-going sort of face, framed by collar-length ginger hair, trimmed with a short beard and soft moustache. It belongs to Ken Scott, a 24-year-old South Londoner who's risen through the ranks of EMI working with The Beatles under George Martin, now employed by Trident as one of its in-house engineers. David's only known him a few months, quickly taking a shine to the laidback manner that belies a meticulous ear for detail – the reason he's offered him the chance to take on what will be Ken's first album as a producer. It also helps that Ken has worked with John Lennon. 'An astounding person,' in David's estimation. 'I adore him.'

It is the most prepared David has ever been. Most of the songs have already been demoed and the band have been rehearsing at home around the foot of the staircase in Haddon Hall for over a week. Songs he likens to 'photostats' of people he knows or admires, of the things they say and the places they go. 'I'm not thinking for myself anymore,' he explains. 'I decided that everything I write sounds very much like what everybody else writes. So I decided to cut out the middleman – me – and go straight to the source of what I'm talking about.'

Mick continues to amaze him, not just as a player but as his new arranger, filling the void left by Tony better than he could have dreamed. David creates such spectacular shoes, but it's Mick who makes them really dance. To see him hunched in the corner of their living room with a pencil and scrap of paper you'd think he was picking out winners from the *Racing Post*, but there sits Haydn of Hull, quietly scoring string parts on the back of an envelope.

Trevor, too, is a revelation. Where other bassists wallow in the sub-octave depths, Trevor comes up for air, playing melodies as he'd parp his trumpet; with Trev in mind, Mick also writes him a real trumpet part for his arrangement of 'Kooks'. And there's Rick Wakeman, who David wishes he could have as his full-time keyboard player if he wasn't already busy in the Strawbs and about to jump ship to become a permanent member of Yes. But, as he did on 'Space Oddity', Rick has the time and the will to lend David his *mezzo forte* fingers once more as a valued session player.

Now the band are all in place. David, hair parted, cans on his ears, stands before the microphone. Ken presses a button and cues 'take one'. The stardust still settling, the *Hunky Dory* tapes roll.

THE ALBUM IS ONLY HALF-DONE when Defries and Laurence send it to the presses. Not as the final LP but as a special promotional record limited to 500 copies – Defries's idea of a black vinyl carrot to tempt open chequebooks in the hustle for that new deal. But Defries being Defries, there's always a catch. Side one of the promo features seven songs by David. The catch is side two: five songs by Dana. She's also been recording at Gem's expense, with David and Mick producing and arranging, including her version of David's 'Andy Warhol'. Defries is gambling on getting them both signed, to the same label, at the same time – the promo, his weapon to enforce his twin pitch.

A fresh batch is hand-delivered to the offices of the main pop papers along with glossy sepia portraits of David, the new ones where he's smoothing back his hair to look like Garbo. Defries's courier is a glitzy wee goblin in silver trousers, a green and silver satin shirt, giant sunglasses and a shaggy feather cut, looking like a cross between Woody Allen and Elton John. He yankee-doodles about David – a close personal friend, doncha know – and how much he loves London. It's just so . . . oh my! . . . *British*! See, he lives in LA where he's A Friend Of The Stars, and that's a fact because, look, he's brought along his scrapbook to prove it. See, that's him grinning with Elvis Presley. And this one's with 'Bobby' – as in Dylan. And that's him with Ringo. And, well, you get the picture. And he's such a hotshot back home he's even had an audience in prison with Charles Manson, so don't believe everything you read because 'Charlie seemed a nice man', although he didn't actually manage to get a buddy pic for his scrapbook. Anyway, LA's not so hot just now because the big new thing is 'taking heroin and dressing sloppy', which is why he loves London so much because it's so cool with all these cute little chicks in hot pants, and T. Rex, and Rod Stewart – oh, man, *every* dude in LA is getting their hair cut like Rod! – and David, of course. Which reminds him, he'd love to stay and talk, but he needs to get back to him . . . hey, did he mention they were great personal friends?

Rodney is in paradise. Or more specifically, Carnaby Street, the King's Road, the Speakeasy, the Marquee, everywhere he's ever read about in imported copies of *Melody Maker*, like he's fallen into its pages and been swallowed up by 'The Raver' column. The Mayor of Sunset Strip is in London superficially on business, earnestly on holy pilgrimage, and personally to see his new girlfriend, Melanie, who he hopes to woo by introducing her to his very great friend, David Bowie. Rodney brings her along to Trident where they watch from the gallery window in the floor of the control room as David sings his own version of 'Andy Warhol'; sparser than Dana's, its eerie intro splicing his studio chat with Ken about how to pronounce *'war-hole'* over malfunctioning computer bleeps just like Jack Nitzsche's spooky synth in *Performance*. After the studio, he takes her out to dinner with David, and Angie, and Defries, who picks up the bill. Then, the following night, Defries invites them out again, just Rodney and Melanie. Yep, he sure knows how to impress a gal, wining and dining with the manager of his very close pal David Bowie. Because Rodney loves the feeling of being useful to Defries, hawking David's promo around the magazine offices, sharing all he knows about the American record industry and offering to hook him up with all his LA contacts. And Melanie, who sits there batting her eyelids not looking at Rodney so much, well, she loves . . . oh . . . now, well . . . And Defries, who smoulders across the table through a caddish cloud of smoke, all thoughts of Dana, never mind Mrs Defries, trickling out of his head like the last drop of wine he chivalrously pours into Melanie's glass, well, he loves . . . he loves . . . oh, well, he loves . . .

WHEN RODNEY FINALLY BOARDS his return flight to LA, he's weighed down with the fabbest of King's Road gear, the hottest discs from the British hit parade and a heart twice as heavy as his suitcase. The Mayor of Sunset Strip. Friend Of The Stars. And a newly single man.

A SINGLE WOMAN, sitting alone, shall not be served after midnight. That's company policy for Empire Catering, owners of London's West End Wimpy bars. Sad unlovable blokes can mope late as they like, pecking at cheeseburgers and Brown Derbys and slurping Rombouts filter coffee. But an unaccompanied lady – by presumption, one of pleasure – must be shown the door without so much as a glass of water. Even if she's a nun.

The nun isn't a nun. The waiters know it, and so does the manager. The same way they can tell that that nurse isn't really a nurse. And that woman over there in the red wig, lace blouse and maxi-skirt isn't a woman but a man in drag. And the man at the opposite table in an oversized suit jacket and drawn-on moustache isn't a man but a woman. And those two, and the other one in the corner, and her – sorry – *him* over there, and how come they're all chanting 'FREE OUR SISTERS!' as one and . . . *oh, bloody hell!*

This, in the Cola Rola summer of '71, is what revolution looks like. Over a hundred Women's Libbers and their system-smashing comrades from the Gay Liberation Front, all dressed up in an all-night Wimpy and no milkshakes to go. They lay siege for over an hour before the police remove them, one by one, many by force, until the manager is forced to shut up early for fear of them coming back. When he does, it's half one in the morning. But the shanty grill suffragettes aren't finished.

A plucky breakaway faction, led by the nun, march onwards from the bottom of Edgware Road to the next nearest all-night branch by Paddington station. More chants, more legs trapped in barricaded doors, more arrests for obstruction. But all these sit-ins and run-ins are not in vain: before winter arrives, victory and 3 a.m. knickerbocker glories shall be theirs. One small step for womankind – but many a giant leap yet to make.

SIXTEEN

THERE ARE MEN IN SPACE AGAIN. It's no longer front-page news, as long as they don't die trying to get there and back, like those three Russians did last month. The crew of *Soyuz 11* spent 24 days in orbit working on the first Soviet space station. On their way home to Earth, a faulty valve caused the air in their capsule to decompress. The automatic re-entry system made a successful splashdown, but when the recovery crew opened the hatch they found Georgi Dobrovolsky, Vadislav Volkov and Viktor Patsayev dead of asphyxiation. The papers named it 'THE COFFIN FROM OUTER SPACE'. They were the first humans to die there.

This time it's the Americans tempting interstellar tragedy. Back in February, they broke the curse of *Apollo 13* when the crew of *Apollo 14* made it to the moon, played golf, and made it home again. The astronauts on *Apollo 15* plan on going one better by becoming the first to drive a moon buggy. NASA nerves fray when the launchpad is struck by lightning, 11 times, but the blast-off goes smoothly at just eight thousandths of a second behind schedule, on course for lunar touchdown approximately 104 hours later. It takes just over four Earth days to reach the moon. A lot of time that could be spent listening to a lot of music.

What records would David take with him if he was on a moonbound rocket?

Stravinsky – *The Rite of Spring*
Biff Rose – *The Thorn in Mrs Rose's Side*
Charles Mingus – *Oh Yeah*
The Beach Boys – *Pet Sounds*
The Beatles – 'She Loves You'

'They all play a substantial part in today's music in the West,' he tells *Mirabelle*'s special moon issue. 'And I like them.'

Just after 6 p.m. on a Friday evening. The night nowhere near dark enough yet to see the moon up above where *Apollo 15*'s Falcon lunar module has just separated from its orbiting command capsule to begin its descent to the surface. Not in Soho, where David smokes a cigarette, staring at nothing in the control room of Trident Studios. Not in Coulsdon, where Terry smokes a cigarette, staring at nothing after eating his tea in the Cane Hill canteen.

Terry. *Oh Yeah*. That was one of his records too. Like David just told the journalist from *Sounds*. 'My brother turned me on to all that.' All that bebop, hard bop, the beatniks. 'The old school.' Terry's world. If David really was on that rocket to the moon, maybe he'd be listening to Mingus, looking out into deep space and thinking of Terry. The way he thinks of him now, glaring down through the studio window: a man stuck in his little capsule, gazing out into the void.

It's the end of the week and the rest of the band have finished and gone for the night. David has hung back on purpose so he can be left alone with his producer. He thinks he has a new song he wants to record, just him on his own, solo. *Thinks*, because even he himself hasn't played it all the way through yet. It's been throbbing in his head all day like a slowly fattening tumour. The tune is simple: a few hippie-ish strumming verses and a chorus using the same chords from the solo bit in 'Moonage Daydream', but looser and sadder. The words are plain barking: pages and pages of what read like stoned scribbled gibberish about pies, gravy and moonboys. Ken asks what it's all about. 'They won't mean anything to you,' says David, which they don't. They mean something only to him. He can't spell it out for everyone because he wants to cut out the middleman – himself – like he does when he writes about other people. Otherwise, he'd have called it 'The Bowie Brothers', instead of knotting the riddle of 'The Bewlay Brothers'. Ken rolls the machines and after five minutes of self-torture in the key of D the tumour is removed. Out of David's head and trapped on tape. Forever.

It is late when they finish. David, emotionally gangbanged, flaps mothlike into Soho's scarlet haze to bathe his bruises in barley wine. Hundreds of thousands of miles above, the gibbous moon glows like a paper cut-out in the blue-black night sky. In another seven spins of the Earth, it will be full and the two earthlings who've just landed there will be almost home again. Back on the same pie'n'gravy planet as David, Terry and the rest of the moonboys.

SEVEN MORE SPINS OF THE EARTH. From the moon, it looks the same as it did seven spins ago, seven hundred spins ago, seven million spins ago. From the porthole of the *Endeavour* command module, still over 24 hours from splashdown off Hawaii, it looks like a giant blue finish line. From the fourth planet from the sun, tens of millions of miles out in the breathless abyss of the solar system, it is only a dim speck in the sky, just as the fourth planet appears in the sky above Earth. A static pinprick of light among thousands and thousands of mostly glimmering pinpricks of light. Would any Martian even bother to wonder: is there life on Earth?

THERE IS. Strange life. Men in robes and wigs who send men who print jokes to jail. An Old Bailey judge convicts the editors of *Oz* magazine to 15 months each for 'conspiracy to corrupt public morals'. Their crime: publishing a 'Schoolkids Issue' sharing contributions from teenage readers, including a cartoon collage pasting the head of Rupert the Bear on a Robert Crumb strip from *Big Ass Comics* about a pervert with a whopping erection forcibly entering a fat virgin. Today's papers steam with liberal outrage over the disproportionately harsh sentences. Apart from anti-porn crusader Mary Whitehouse – Heinrich Himmler trapped in the drag of a Dick Emery spinster – who thinks their punishment 'is about right'. In gratitude, *Oz*'s sister paper, *Ink*, invites cartoonist Gerald Scarfe to immortalise Whitehouse on their next cover: lying on her back, in front of the Pope, legs apart, being pumped by Rupert the Bear. Strange, strange, strange life.

Stranger life still. Sexy girls in T-shirts bearing Japanese demon faces that go *bleep!* when the nose is pressed. Satin coats decorated with cotton discs filled with butterflies, brocade jumpsuits with bloody scenes of hara-kiri, skirts hemmed with dragon teeth, peacock feather jackets, quilted kimonos, red lacquer platform boots and giant capes with tongue-poking samurais. New fashions from 27-year-old Tokyo designer Kansai Yamamoto, now in London selling his cheaper designs in Biba and his most marvellous, and expensive, in a boutique on the Fulham Road. 'Soon, fashion will have an international feeling,' says Kansai, 'and it will be the Eastern people who give it impetus.' Bold, exotic, colourful life.

Bolder life still. Shiny underpants with a skull and eagle wings sewed on the crotch, leather boots imprinted with the same insignia, a glittering gold cape and a peroxide blond Viking mane. Typically seen on a Saturday afternoon pinning Honey Boy Zimba to the canvas of a Bradford wrestling ring on *World of Sport*. Adrian Street – 'the Liberace of the leg hold' – is the Welsh son of a miner from Brynmawr who believes he is spiritually descended from Ancient Greece. That's why he owns 250 toy Greek soldiers, an oil painting of Alexander the Great and a wardrobe fit for Zeus: over 20 jackets and dressing gowns, garish satins and silks, bejewelled with sequins and rhinestones. 'People think I'm a showman,' says Street, 'but I'm not. I'm just conceited.' Loud, vain, glamorous life.

Louder life still. Friday morning ears ring from last night's *Top of the Pops*. 'WELL ALLLRIGHT EVERYBOOODDDDDDDY!' Where Mott The Hoople fail, Slade succeed as the band who really *can* bottle a live riot on record. A week ago, they wore out the whistles of Fife constabulary when a packed-out youth club gig in St Andrews was besieged by 500 extra fans from the wrong side of the Tay Bridge. To be expected when you make Bash Street bovver-rock fit for Dundee heid-the-baws. 'Get Down And Get With It' is their first Top 20 hit after growing out their skinheads and beating the living daylights out of a little-known Little Richard tune. The *NME* file them under the 'Me, Tarzan – You, Jane' school of rock'n'roll. A fair cop, says bonneted boss Noddy Holder. 'Me and our mates are just a bunch of ravers. Black Sabbath are the same as us – Black Country yobbos. We like being like that. We don't care if we are a bunch of yobbos. We are what we are, if ya know what I mean.' The kids know, even if the critics don't. Crazee, noizee, rollicking life.

Crazee-er life still. In sleepy Maida Vale, where the fat branches of plane trees poke towards the sky like cheerleaders shaking leafy pompoms, Marc Bolan starts the day with a glass of 'breakfast wine'. Normal behaviour when you've had your second number 1. 'Get It On' has been there for three weeks already and will stay there one more. The new T. Rex album, *Electric Warrior*, is out next month and Marc thinks – no, he *knows* – it's a masterpiece. 'I don't see how you could be disappointed with it.' Then there's his cosmic messiah film which he tells this week's *Jackie* is definitely still happening. 'The script centres around a character from outer space whose superior knowledge comes to help people with their problems.' Alien, interplanetary, fantastic life. Right here on Earth. Thirty-three million miles from a red planet that cannot hear us, nor really see us. Just the pinprick of light.

It takes three minutes for the light from Mars to reach the Earth. From first word to last, the time it takes for David to sing his song about an unhappy girl, fed up and stood up, alone in the cinema, jaded by the meaninglessness of the flickering images up on the screen. The same *'Sai-lors!'* song that came to him that day in Bec Rec park. The melody is borrowed, which he doesn't deny. Three years, one manager and who knows how many hairstyles ago he'd been encouraged to submit some English lyrics for a French tune, 'Comme D'Habitude'. They weren't very good, and as the record shows, he took the blows, and Paul Anka beat him with 'My Way'. Today in Trident – as the men from *Oz* pray for appeal in their Wormwood Scrubs cells, as Sombrero Wendy flicks through the new *Vogue* with its 'GLAMAMOTO' Yamamoto spread, as Adrian Street ponders which sparkles to wear for tomorrow's live televised bout in Watford, as Slade's van brums along the A449 on their way to shake the plaster off the ceiling of Blackwood Miners' Institute, as number 1 Marc pours another glass of breakfast wine – David gets to rewrite history. The same Sinatra tune, but with better words than his failed first draft. 'My Way', his way.

His is a dreamer's, not a survivor's, song. It looks up, not back. The words act like stage directions for the music to supply the drama. A symphony of folding velvet seats, dimming house lights, the spotlit dust sinking slowly through the ray of the projector, the stale smell of sugar and tobacco, the curtain drawing back, trailers for 'OUR NEXT FEATURE PRESENTATION', the sparks from the RKO Radio Pictures transmitter tower reflecting in the eyes of the girl with the clearest view.

The dialogue is David's, but the action is Mick's. He scores strings that yearn with Garbo loneliness, stranded and hopeless, like gazing at the stars through the sodium streetlight of a Hull council estate. *Adagio sostenuto.* The romantic suspense of Rachmaninov, the crescendos and kettle drums of Richard Strauss. All will be added later, but Mick conducts the band as if the orchestra's there with them. Trevor and Woody, kept waiting for the choruses to throw their weight. Rick, flourishing Chopin cadenzas on the same Bechstein concert grand McCartney used on 'Hey Jude'. And Mick's own electric touch, brief and precise as the twilight sputters of falling meteors. An amphitheatre for David to make high opera of a desperate young soul lost *at*, not in, the pictures. A love song to shooting star wishers. And the climax – *allargando* – a supernova of . . .

Brrring! Brrring!

Rick crashes in the last bar.

Brrring! Brrring!

Next to his piano is the downstairs studio toilet. In the toilet, a wall-mounted payphone which hardly ever rings. But as the piano mics pick up, it's ringing now.

Brrring! Brrring!

The take is ruined. Mick despairs. 'Fookin' bastard!'

Brrring! Brrring!

'Aw . . . FOR FOOKSAKE!'

Ken, sighing, stops the tape and spools it back to the beginning. David and the band take a minute to compose themselves. A new cue. 'Take two.' And again, the symphony, the yearning, the weight, the cadenzas, the meteors, the opera, the supernova. This time, nobody rings.

Somewhere over a hundred thousand miles above, the crew of *Apollo 15* are woken from their space sleep by Mission Control with the sailors' song 'Anchors Aweigh'. A day from home, they eat their last meals of wet-pack beef stew and rehydratable grape punch after taking some photos of the lunar eclipse. From the porthole of their capsule the full moon is a burnt orange colour. From Earth, it's a paler orange, but still not the most interesting feature in tonight's clear sky. That's the red planet: blazing fiery bright, high above the horizon. The closest it's been to Earth for 47 years in fact.

It had to be. This day, of all days, when David records 'Life On Mars?'

SEVENTEEN

THE POSTER GIVES CLEAR WARNING. 'This play has explicit sexual content and "offensive" language. If you are likely to be disturbed, please do not attend. MATURE ADULTS ONLY!' The mature British adults of the British press aren't offended, just exasperated. 'TOP OF THE FLOPS' yawns the *Mirror* headline, *'as boring as a plate of baked beans'*. The upright *Times* shivers and damns it *'a witless, invertebrate mind-numbing farrago'*. Even the streetwise counterculture vultures at *Time Out* are deflated: *'Plays have to be written. Otherwise, they are a bore. Like this.'*

The sexually explicit bore is *Andy Warhol's Pork*. It's touted as Andy's first theatrical production, though he didn't actually *write* it, just as he didn't actually direct last year's *Andy Warhol's Flesh* or this year's *Andy Warhol's Trash*. The play only gets his branding because he recorded the telephone conversations the script is based on, which his secretary then transcribed and which an off-Broadway actor and director named Tony Ingrassia sieved for the most outrageous highlights to string together as an 'experimental' drama. That's if you can call *Pork* a drama. It's really more of an elaborate in-joke about Andy and his circle of friends, each thinly veiled among its cast of camp caricatures. Andy is the impassive voyeur 'B. Marlowe'. Andy's film director Paul Morrissey is 'Pall'. Andy's boyfriend Jed and his twin brother Jay are 'the Pepsodent Twins'. Warhol superstar Viva is 'Vulva Lips'. And the title character,

113

'Amanda Pork', is another of his superstars, the plump socialite Brigid Berlin, nicknamed 'Brigid Polk' because she's always poking herself with 'vitamin' injections of speed – or 'Vita-meata-vegamin' as it becomes in the play. A lot of the actors spend a lot of their time naked, some with spray-painted pubic hair, pretending to masturbate with kitchen whisks, or demonstrating a 'plate job', involving a male cast member lying naked on the floor with a Pyrex glass dish over his face so he can watch a woman 'shit' on top of him: they substitute with blobs of chocolate pudding. When a heckler is thrown out after standing up and screaming 'This is the biggest dose of crap I've seen in my life!' nobody can be sure they didn't mean it literally.

Pork has just opened for a month's run at the Roundhouse, every night Monday to Thursday and twice on Fridays and Saturdays. It's only its second production after it premiered in early May in a Downtown Manhattan theatre, closing after two weeks and a half-decent review in the *New York Times* calling it *'occasionally revolting but more often good, dirty fun'*: the *Village Voice* found it altogether *'hateful'*. Andy was disappointed they couldn't transfer to Broadway, but took solace from his English dealer, Ira Gale, who offered to bring it to London instead. So here it is.

And here they are, *Pork*'s New York cast and crew, billeted in a mansion flat in Earl's Court where they pop mandies, drop acid and fuck rent boys picked up from the local tube station. They include the assistant director Leee Black Childers, a charming gay Kentuckian who fell into Andy's world photographing Downtown drag queens; actual drag queen and fellow Southern boy Wayne County, the redeeming star of the show for most critics; and gay actor Tony Zanetta, known as 'Zee', resuming the Warhol role of B. Marlowe for which he's dyed and chopped his hair to mimic Andy's trademark silvery mop.

Also living there is the new Amanda Pork. Since nobody was happy with the original casting, the London production introduces New York groupie Kathy Dorritie in the role. Kathy was raised a Catholic, which is justifiable reason for any woman to dedicate her life, as she has, to the blessed vengeance of casual sex mania. Besides acting, she's currently hustling to write her own column in the American rock magazine *Circus* under the pen name 'Cherry Vanilla' – 'CHERRY VANILLA WITH

SCOOPS FOR YOU' – an alter-ego itching to overwhelm her at the first opportunity.

It's a Wednesday night in Camden. The whisk orgasm over, the chocolate pudding splatted, another queasy, titillated and underwhelmed audience pours out of the Roundhouse. For the *Pork* cast the day of night at last begins. Usually that means the Speakeasy, or the Marquee, or their favourite retreat, the newly opened Hard Rock Café on Old Park Lane, where they can flap and squawk as loud as they like enjoying a proper American burger instead of that limp limey crap they serve in Wimpy bars. But not tonight. Leee's eyes have been alerted to an advert for a gig just up the hill from the Roundhouse in Belsize Park, somewhere called the Country Club. 'A transvestite singer' is how he sells it to Kathy and Wayne who agree to go with him – the one he remembers reading about a few months ago in the same issue of *Rolling Stone* with Andy's actor Joe Dallesandro on the cover and a big interview with Andy's director Paul Morrissey inside. It stuck in his head because this singer – this transvestite – said something outrageous about wanting to be found in bed with Raquel Welch's husband and wore a dress in the accompanying photo. He sounds very gay. Very them. Very Andy.

'**DAAAVIIID!**' Angie tsunamis into the pantry that passes for the Country Club's backstage dressing room.

'The cast of *Pork* are here! *ANDY WARHOL'S PORK!*'

David stops tuning his guitar. Did she say *Warhol*?

'They've heard about you! They're sitting out in front now. Three of them. Isn't that FABULOUS?'

The Country Club isn't what Leee, Wayne and Kathy expect. They find it, just, down a dead-end alleyway opposite the Odeon cinema on Haverstock Hill, hustling their way in for free thanks to their accents, all that's needed to authenticate a bullshit story about being a party of US rock critics there to review the show. Once inside, they quickly process it for the kind of hippie dump they'd avoid like rabies back in the Village: a small room with a low ceiling, an inch-high stage at one end and a couple of dozen kids sitting, squatting or leaning disinterestedly

115

against the wall. Apart from a butch whirling dervish impossible to ignore with an even louder American accent than theirs: Angie in full cyclone. To their surprise they discover she's the transvestite's wife – so maybe he *isn't* so gay, and maybe she *isn't* a lesbian as they assumed ten seconds ago?

They chance introducing themselves properly.

Angie pops.

'OH! HE'LL BE *THRILLED* WHEN I TELL HIM! YOU MUST STICK AROUND AFTER THE SHOW!'

The transvestite turns out to be not so much of a transvestite – long hair, a baggy blouse, baggier trousers and no lipstick. He's joined by a cute blond guitar player and a not-so-cute six-foot hippie piano player. It's all a bit too drippy-sounding for Leee and Wayne, though Kathy likes it, listening as she is with her eyes to the pleasant melody of the blond guitarist's trousers.

It's near the end, before he plays 'Andy Warhol', when David acknowledges their presence.

'Some friends of Andy Warhol are here with us tonight. Where are they?'

The trio make themselves known. Leee stands, flapping his eyelids like a dowager's fan. Wayne curtseys. Kathy pulls her top down to one side and flashes a tit. In the second it takes to pop it back again, her transformation is complete. Kathy Dorritie, as listed in the programme of *Pork*, is dead. Cherry Vanilla has taken over.

As dragooned by Angie, they hover back to meet David after he's finished. He turns out to be really very charming, and really very interested in hearing about their work with Andy. Leee says he'll arrange tickets for them to come and see *Pork*. Angie makes it a date. On the long trek home to the Earl's Court flat they've lovingly christened 'Pig Mansions', stoned opinions settle. They agree David and Angie 'seem like lovely people'. That David was 'cute' but nothing like the tarted-up queen they'd been led to believe, even if he did have long hair and Mary Jane shoes. That his music was 'too folky' and Andy would probably hate it. And that his wife very obviously wore the pants.

'Who, *butch*?'

'Yeah!'

'Oh, no doubt. That Angie – she *runs* the fucking show.'

IT'S LIKE THEY'VE SUDDENLY SLIPPED through time and space and ended up back in New York in the backroom of Max's Kansas City. Queens, poseurs, hustlers, scores, hookers, daddies, aunties, fast broads and fairy princesses. A heaven from heaven home from home. All these weeks they've been here in London – how come *nobody* told them about the Sombrero?

David and Angie proudly show the *Pork* drove their kingdom, a favour returned for the previous evening when they were treated to two hours of wild, perverted, speedballing Warholia as guests at the Roundhouse. Afterwards they met the rest of the cast, including its fake Andy, Tony 'Zee', here tonight with Leee, Wayne and Cherry, conspicuous strangers in the piss-elegant court of Freddie, Wendy and the other beautiful dolls.

So is Mick, choking on his beer as he tries to swat Cherry's groping paws out of his crotch. This is after she's flashed him her tits. Twice. Angie sees the distress signals throbbing on Mick's cheeks, and takes action. She snatches Cherry's hand – 'HEY! COME WITH ME!' – pulling her off to the dancefloor. The music is fast and funky.

'Treat her like!'

Angie leads, their bodies bumping, pelvis to pelvis, breast to breast. Gently at first, then harder, more regular.

'Gotta treat her like!'

Cherry giggles. So that's the game: make out on the floor like a couple of dykes?

'Treat her like!'

Angie shoots her a pout. Cherry shimmies round and bends over, grinding backwards into Angie, tongue lolling, hands running sensuously through her hair. The other dancers, too self-absorbed to care, pay no attention.

'Treat her like a lady!'

For Cherry, it's all a delicious blasphemy. *Bless me, Father, for I have cavorted in public with fallen women and sodomites to the Devil's own Cornelius Brothers and loved every second, A-fucking-men!*

117

For Angie, a friendly war dance. Every bump, every slap, every fondle is its own territorial display. *Cute, but tread careful, sister! Don't let me catch those wayward mitts of yours anywhere near my husband's crotch. Just remember who's boss – remember who runs the fucking show!*

Mick watches them slip'n'slide from the booth, a daft smile on his face hammered there by alcohol and being a million light years from Hull. Beside him, Freddie's eyes flit elsewhere, man to man, groin to groin, up each leg and down again, muttering a running commentary as if broadcasting live to his imaginary listeners of Radio Polari.

'Hmm . . . bona lallies . . . and aren't we just *bursting* out of our basket? . . . . oh, but *far* too much slap on that eek, dear! . . . someone tell that homi-polone to go home and rinse out her tights, the cod queen . . .'

Opposite, oblivious, David is in private conference with Zee. He wants to know everything there is to know about Andy that he doesn't already, and interrogating the pretend Andy seems a good place to start. Zee tries to tell him all he can, which is too much to tell in one night in a loud gay discotheque, seated next to radio Freddie while Angie, Cherry, Leee and Wayne divebomb back and forth for more drinks.

The conversation resumes the next day at Haddon Hall where Zee, alone, is specially ferried to David's door in a prepaid minicab. Angie plays hostess as Zee entertains David for hours: about Andy, what he's like in the cold flesh; how weird he was when he came to *Pork* rehearsals and found himself talking to himself, each Andy trying to out-bore the other in the same deadpan 'uh' voice; his studio, the Factory, and the crazy freaks who hang out there; and Max's, the restaurant over the street where they all hang out in the backroom, sort of their equivalent of the Sombrero.

David plays Zee tapes of his new songs. In particular, he wants him to hear 'Andy Warhol'. 'I decided to stop singing about myself,' says David. 'I used to be the most serious of serious people, coming out with great drooling nine-minute epics which were really tedious and boring. But my material has become a lot lighter since I came back from the States. Now I write about anything that comes to mind. Picking up on what other people say, writing it down and making songs out of it.'

Zee understands. The art of the impassive voyeur. It's only later that night, back in Pig Mansions talking to Cherry and his friends, spilling the beans on his daytrip to Beckenham when Zee realises – all that time talking together, David told him nothing of any real substance about himself whatsoever.

How *very* Andy.

ANDY SLEEPS. Like a king, in a four-poster bed, a tiger-skin rug laid in front, two floors above street level in the Upper East Side townhouse he'd shared with his 79-year-old mother until a few months ago when she returned to the care of his brother's family in Pittsburgh. Outside, the leaves on the pear tree hang tight to their branches, hungry for the coming Manhattan sun. The city of night draws its curtain. Hosed sidewalks, boiler steam and the tommy gun *rrllrllrrll* of rising shop shutters. Dawn's pigeons peck in trash cans and joggers emerge from the violet haze of Central Park. Buses, delivery trucks and yellow cabs tune up the traffic for the carbon monoxide symphony to come. Another summer's day in New York City.

The heat hasn't reached its slimy nylon peak when Tony Defries leaves his hotel and hails a cab. A man on a mission, he doesn't even notice the strange, bearded busker dressed a bit like a Viking, eyes closed, cloak wrapped tightly around his shoulders, standing where he always stands at the corner of the Warwick on 54th. Andy would: back in the late Fifties he designed Moondog's first album cover. So would his mother: she did the lettering.

Defries has been in town for nearly a week already, armed with copies of the David and Dana promo record and a gab honed slicker than Mephistopheles. It helps that the wind of American record retail is blowing in his and David's favour. So far, it's been the Year of the Singer-Songwriter: Carole King's *Tapestry* unshiftable at number 1 and James Taylor selling out three nights at Carnegie Hall *and* on the cover of *Time* magazine. The English pop dollar is also strong: the Stones ever invincible, Elton still flying high, Rod Stewart now in his slipstream and the Bee Gees' new single America's number 1. Defries sees his timing as perfect – a once-in-a-lifetime offer to sign the next big English singer-songwriter superstar. And don't just take his word for it – read what it said in a round-up of young British talent in last month's *New York Times*.

'The day will come when David Bowie is a star and the crushed remains of his melodies are broadcast from Muzak boxes in every elevator and hotel lobby in town.'

Defries's destination is ten gridlocked blocks south, a recently completed 45-storey skyscraper off Times Square and the new home to RCA Victor. Fifteen years ago, they had the record industry all sewn up in the golden thread of Elvis Presley, theirs the black labels with the gramophone hound that first rocked the stars and rolled the stripes. Elvis still sells for them, even when they repackage his old hits in tacky triple LP box sets with free scraps of cloth supposedly 'cut from Elvis's own wardrobe!' They also remain the biggest popular country music label, home to Dolly Parton, Charley Pride and their latest big hitter, John Denver. But when it comes to rock and pop, RCA's quota is pitiful, and they know it. Which is why they've just hired a new Chosen One to yank them into the Seventies.

His name is Dennis Katz, a young lawyer who, according to his former bosses at Columbia Records, owns 'an innate sophistication for what is good and what is bad in rock music'. The same sadly doesn't apply to his choice of knitwear. As RCA's gaudy-sweatered Division Vice President of Contemporary Music, Dennis vows to 'get into the street': the words aren't long out of his mouth when he goes and signs The Everly Brothers. But he also wants 'writer-performers' and 'artists unique in their approach'. Soft or hard rock, it doesn't matter. Dennis's motto: 'If it's good – I'll take it!'

Defries is the very man Dennis has been waiting to walk into his office since his name went on the door in April. He listens to his visitor's pitch like a cobra to the toot of an Indian pungi. A writer-performer who can help RCA create a new contemporary music image for the label? Dennis is keen before he's heard a note. Defries leaves him a copy of the promo record. Dennis promises to play it – *both* sides – and think it over. That weekend, Mrs Katz makes his mind up for him. She loves it. That means it's good. And if it's good – as Don and Phil Everly well know – Dennis takes it.

Back on Sixth Avenue, he telephones Defries's hotel to break the good news. 'David's a very exciting talent,' says Dennis. 'I'd like to offer you a deal.'

The line is eerily quiet. A second frozen in the static silence of victory. 'OK,' says Defries. 'And what about Dana?'

Up on Lexington, the pear tree gorges on the city heat. Andy isn't home and Moondog isn't on his corner. Another copy of *Tapestry* is sold in King Karol on 42nd Street and a Greenwich Village matinee of *Bananas* changes reels. A Midtown exchange operator patches a long-distance call through to Beckenham, England, to let someone with the same birthday as Elvis Presley know that they're now also on the same record label. And five hours ahead and an ocean away, in the Kensington basement nicknamed 'the Bunker', the telephone doesn't ring.

EIGHTEEN

'**BY THE WAY,** if you don't know, I'm Marc Bolan. You've seen me on *Top of the Pops*, right?' Jeers and beer cans catapult towards the stage. Not the headliner's welcome T. Rex expected, but then nothing about the Weeley Festival has so far gone according to plan. It's been hyped as 'the Festival for the Fans', or this year's equivalent of last year's Isle of Wight: tens of thousands of kids risking crabs and cholera to hear the biggest names in rock electrifying the fields outside a village in Essex over the August bank holiday weekend. Weeley's organisers have the added brainwave of scheduling the music without any zodiacal consultation: to run non-stop from late on Friday to dawn the following Monday. A brave and, as the heavens foretell, impossible plan.

After eight hours of waiting to go on stage, Curved Air strop homewards without taking their see-thru violin out of its case. Mott The Hoople's midnight slot becomes a 5 a.m. sleepwalk, so bad Ian Hunter apologises to those half-watching in a similar state of near collapse. Changeovers are tortuously long and vibe-stranglingly silent. A side-of-stage record deck is arranged but not an actual DJ; when they finally find one his records are stolen before he can play any. Ignoring all of history's warnings from Altamont, the security is recruited from Essex Hells Angels who take it upon themselves to smash up the concession stalls. The traders retaliate with their own heavy mob and in the thump of an axe handle the mud is littered with groaning young men, bloody denim and Maltese crosses. Three tents burn down, their occupants rushed to hospital. And long, long before Marc reaches the stage, sanitation has deteriorated to that of a refugee camp squatting on a rubbish dump.

As the Sunday sun sets, Weeley seems a battle not worth winning but the Faces are here to conquer regardless. Rod Stewart arrives on site in a white Rolls-Royce, stepping out in a pink satin Mr Freedom suit, exactly like the one Jagger wore on *Top of the Pops*, a matching pink neck scarf and no shirt: half man, half Mr Kipling French Fancy, with a cockatoo crown he puts down to 'six years of torturing the barnet'. The band's entourage includes a designated 'wine roadie' whose job it is to chill the Blue Nun to their desired temperature. 'Well,' justifies Rod, 'we deserve a bit of luxury.' Whether because of the clobber, the tunes or the tangible magic of Liebfraumilch, the crowd can't get enough, nor the critics who unanimously hail the Faces Kings of Weeley by an Essex mile. 'Here's a song 'bout a schoolboy what falls in love with a dirty old prostitute,' Rod announces before strutting into 'Maggie May'. In another six weeks it will be top of the charts on both sides of the Atlantic. The field rejoices like it already is.

Marc *was* top of the UK charts until two weeks ago. Now it's Diana Ross with 'I'm Still Waiting', her first British solo number 1, all thanks to Tony Blackburn's relentless airplay of an older LP track forcing Motown to issue it as a single. Sweet symphonic soul about being a fool for love, the ideal soundtrack for eligible bachelors pecking at another plate of tinned salmon, gazing sadly into the distance beyond a reproduction *Hay Wain*. Looking around Weeley at the last lairy geezers standing – cans of Party Seven, ripped denims, uniform collar-length hair like Adam Faith's in *Budgie* – it's a safe bet not many here would have bought it. Judging from Marc's reception, possibly not 'Get It On' either.

Like Rod, he opts for satin, a plain jacket open over a £4 Chuck Berry T-shirt from Mr Freedom. Unlike Rod, after his first number he hears a cry from the front, piercing the air like a perfectly aimed harpoon.

'*FUCK OFF!*'

Marc grips his mic, ears leading his eyes to the spot where it came from.

'Why don't *YOU* fuck off?'

But somewhere in a field of philistines beats at least one glitter heart. A week later, the *Melody Maker* mailbag hears its thump.

'*During the Weeley pop festival I realised just how snobbish some progressive music fans are. When T. Rex appeared, they were hailed with much booing and abuse from the self-appointed pop intellectuals . . . Don't worry, Marc, for to quote Sun-Ra, "booing is the sound of sub-humans."*'

THE SOUND OF SO MANY SUBWAYS AND HUMANS combines in a low, droning constant B flat. The keynote of New York City, same as it was when David first felt it eight months ago. All that's changed is the humidity, the daylight, the names of the films on the cinema hoardings and the songs on the radio. It's warmer, and stickier. The sun sets around seven, on clear nights draping Manhattan in a smoky veil of amber. The signs for *Diary of a Mad Housewife* now say *The Anderson Tapes* and you can't touch a dial without hearing Carole King the way it was with Elton John. The Electric Circus where David met the man who wasn't Lou Reed is now gone, as has the Gaslight Café where he saw Tim Hardin, and the Fillmore East where Marc saw red. But the sidewalks still crackle with the voltage of so much humanity dangerously unearthed. Garbo still skulks through Midtown in her arm's-length armour of sunglasses and headscarf. The wooden Indian chief outside Nat Sherman's still welcomes smokers over its threshold with cold carved eyes dead as cancer. The Met still charges a discretional one dollar to gawp at El Greco. Philip Glass's cab meter still ticks nervously to the Bronx and back. You can still buy three-buck junk if you know which pizza parlour to score outside. Muggers still mug, pimps still pimp, hustlers still hustle, and as from next week the new season of *Alias Smith and Jones* is back in its regular slot on Thursdays at 8 p.m. Still the city of night, and of Andy, and 'I'm Waiting For The Man', and Birdland, and Ratso Rizzo. Still *his* New York.

If anything, a richer New York because he's in a richer hotel. The Warwick, on Moondog's corner of 54th and Sixth. Defries's idea, to book them into the same suite where The Beatles used to stay, starting as he means David's career to go on: from the top, and upwards.

As far as David understands, his new label are paying for it, which is why he's here, to formally sign the RCA deal. It happens in their Sixth

Avenue boardroom under an old B-movie poster for *Bulldog Drummond's Revenge*, with Dennis, in a cowboy shirt, and other close-shaven men in suits smelling of fresh dry cleaning, mouthwash and mistresses. David wears a black fedora, black culottes and a tight paisley shirt decorated with astrological brooches. He smells of Alvin Toffler's *Future Shock*, sex and cigarettes. Defries is casual in a T-shirt and jeans and a fat stogie clamped in his jaw making him smell of Al Capone. Without it, he'd still smell of Al Capone. A pen is uncapped, David's hand sweeps, ink skates and, in a silent Faustian thunderclap, dries. Hands are shaken and commemorative flashbulbs pop. Defries's smoke curls up past the barrel tip of Bulldog Drummond's gun; it looks like he's just fired it.

David Bowie has signed to RCA to record three albums for them in the next two years, with an option to extend. He'll be advanced $37,500 per album – split with Defries, minus expenses, the bill for several nights' luxury in the presidential suite at the Warwick quite possibly included. David's welcome gifts from his new bosses include the entire back catalogue of Elvis Presley and a celebration meal at the Ginger Man, a restaurant on the Upper West Side popular with the Met Opera crowd, famed for its posh decor and cheap omelettes.

As an added surprise, the suits from RCA invite along another singer-songwriter they've just picked up, about to make his first solo album since quitting his old band a year ago. He arrives skipping out of a sudden downpour, hands flicking droplets from dark curls grown halfway to Marc length, wearing a black leather jacket, scruffy top and jeans. He smells of graffiti, needles and rock'n'roll. Somebody else speaks and fate stutters.

'David – this is Lou.'

This is Lou. *The* Lou. Not the Doug Yule 'look, buddy' wrong Lou he met eight months ago but *the actual* Lewis Allan Reed, former singer with The Velvet Underground, friend of Warhol, bard of white light, Stutz Bearcats and Lexington 1-2-5. Sitting opposite him now, with those giant unblinking toadlike eyes of his, their pupils an infinity of fuckyous, their whites vibrating with the last amps of electroshock he suffered as a teenager as the only suggested cure for being born Lou Reed. Which clearly didn't work because here he is, 29 and still as Louishly Lou as the psychiatrists feared even before he'd hissed a line of 'The Black Angel Death Song'.

David takes a nervous gulp of wine. Lou orders a Scotch and smiles over the tablecloth with his steamrolled pucker of a mouth. David's fangs flash back. Lou starts to speak in a voice straight off the Haddon Hall record deck. Outside, a rain shower spatters romantically against the windowpanes, washing the last dregs of reality into the gutter. This night no longer has need for it.

A **SECOND LIGHTNING BOLT** waits to strike. Downtown. A spacious loft apartment a few blocks south of the Flatiron. There's a figure sunk on a couch, hypnotised by the monochrome flickers of a television set showing how good life ought to be if it was all in soft focus and time ticked to the gloopy sweet strings of 'Jeanie With The Light Brown Hair'. His own life is not this good, which is why he's watching this version, to forget that he's a homeless 24-year-old heroin addict, $10,000 in debt to the record label who've just dumped him and his band – a band who've since broken up, being skint, fucked and largely insane. His habit is raging, his prospects bleak, but his spirit remains unbreakable. If the bomb went off and he was the last man left on Earth, just him and the cockroaches, he'd dust himself off and form a band with the cockroaches. Iggy's a syringe half-full kind of guy.

'Iggy?'

He hears his name but chooses to ignore it. Don't interrupt, not while Jimmy Stewart's being so goddamn sincere. Any minute now he'll be talking about his dad. *'He used to say to me, "Have you ever noticed how grateful you are to see daylight again after coming through a long dark tunnel?"'* Aw, Jimmy kills him. *'Well, he'd say, "Always try to see life around you as if you'd just come out of a tunnel."'* Isn't that just fucking beautiful?

'*Iggy?*'

The voice belongs to his friend and manager, Danny Fields. This is his apartment. That's his couch Iggy's sprawled on and his electricity bill feeding the TV that's breaking Iggy's heart with *Mr. Smith Goes to Washington*.

'IGGY?'

He sighs. Danny has his attention.

'C'mon. We're going to Max's.'

Iggy's eyebrows shoot up. Then shoot back down. He isn't keen. It's late and besides he'd rather stay here watching Jimmy Stewart, *'an honorary stooge'* fighting The Man. But Danny insists. There's someone he 'has' to meet. Someone who wants to meet *him*. Danny's journalist friend, Lisa, whose husband works for RCA, just rang to tell them he's on his way to Max's now.

'The one who mentioned you in the *New Musical Express* – remember I showed you?'

He does. Vaguely. A few months back. One of the imported English papers ran a poll asking singers to name their Top 3 favourite singers. Neil Young came out first, John Lennon second. Marc's choice was Jim Morrison. And then there was the guy who listed his number 1 as 'Iggy Pop'. Nobody in the English papers mentioned Iggy *ever*. Except this 'David Bowie'.

'He's been nice about you. C'mon?'

Iggy turns from the TV to Danny, then back to the TV. Jimmy Stewart's shiny big boy scout eyes beseech him. *Son, don't miss the wonders that surround you.*

'Aw . . .'

Iggy leaves Mr Smith on Capitol Hill and walks with Mr Fields the four short blocks to Max's. If only to see what life looks like outside the tunnel.

STEAK, LOBSTER, CHICKPEAS. The spotlit Park Avenue promise outside Max's Kansas City. The steak and the lobster are house specialities. The dried chickpeas are free, a bowl on each table, intended as bar snacks but so tough the only time anyone ever touches one isn't to eat it but to throw it. There isn't a Max either, and the restaurant has no connection to Kansas City other than the most expensive steak on the menu. It's run by a local restaurateur named Mickey who opened it six years ago with the dream of creating an artists' bar. Inside, it's a cross between a gallery and a steakhouse where short-skirted waitresses buzz around abstract canvasses and crushed metal sculptures, all of it donated by artists, like Andy, to cover their bar tab. Andy comes less these days, but when he does, he still likes his regular table in the Back Room, where Hell is a place on Earth and the Devil a drag queen laughing in the bloody glow of its red neon cross.

David, blinking crimson disbelief, sits with the last of the RCA party. Spacewalk drunk on meeting Lou – since gone home – being in Andy's place – though Andy isn't in tonight – and the sight of the laughing timebomb skipping towards his table. *Tick, tick, boom!*

'David? I'm Iggy.'

Iggy. So, he's real: real as Lou, only David never had any trouble imagining Lou as being an actual person. But Iggy – the name alone – he was always straight out of a comic book. He even *looks* drawn: the boomerang smile, the gobstopper eyes threatening to balloon out of their sockets, a weird restless alien lifeforce zapped here from planet Ig. Grinning at David. Not a hostile grin, just plain amused. That this spook-eyed Veronica Lake is his number 1 English fan. The one he dumped Jimmy Stewart for.

Night stretches and the unreal city exhales. Those who worry about time are already in bed; those who don't have already forgotten it two chasers ago. In Max's neon cross, electrons tremble and photons fizz. Beyond it, lips move, and David and Iggy melt as one in the beautiful scarlet saturation.

DAWN DOES NOT SEPARATE THEM LONG. Iggy joins David and Defries in their hotel suite, surrounded by room service trolleys. They offer him 'breakfast'. He orders two. As he forks down eggs and hash browns he tells them the sorry tale of the little boy from a trailer park in Ann Arbor, Michigan, born James Newell Osterberg Jr, and his band, The Stooges: how only a few months ago they fell to pieces after two albums – damn fucking cool albums too, as David knows – just as he'd started writing with a savage new guitarist from Texas called James Williamson; how he's fucked, in debt to his old label, unable to get a new one, but he's got it all in hand, see, as he's now with a methadone clinic and that luminous green shit's going to help him kick the junk once and for all. And, gee, this is awful swell, and don't suppose he could get *another* breakfast sent up?

David says Iggy should come over to England. Hire fresh musicians and start a new band there. Iggy shakes his head. He can't leave his writing partner, this kid James. They come as a team.

A ripple of cigar smoke wafts from Defries's mouth as he removes it to speak. 'I understand,' he says, light as cream. 'And I can help. Let me manage you.' He takes a soft puff. 'I can get you a record deal. You go back home, work on your songs with your friend. Finish your methadone programme. Let me take care of everything.'

David watches for a response. Defries quietly replaces his cigar and emits another silent cloud. Like a choo-choo train – thinks Iggy, beaming – that's just pulled him out of his tunnel.

NINETEEN

DAVID, LOU AND IGGY. Time and space don't seem big enough to hold the three of them, but New York is its own quantum dimension.

He sees Lou again, at another dinner party thrown by Lisa, the journalist who called Danny to bring Iggy to Max's, and her husband Richard, who's going to produce Lou's album. The Robinson's Upper West Side apartment is painted in Powis Square maroons and browns in homage to Jagger's pad in *Performance*. David feels instantly at home. Encouraged, he and Lou play their own game of Turner and Chas, picking up where they left off the other night at the restaurant, slipping away to a bedroom where they lock the door. Some conversations are just much too precious to be disturbed.

But even New York has only so much time and so much space. Don't squeeze too hard or it'll backfire and take your head off like a badly loaded gun. The knack is knowing when to say 'when'. David might, but Defries definitely doesn't. Too much is never enough. He wants Andy.

Defries has an in. Zee, the fake Andy from *Pork*, lives a few blocks west of Max's. He's summoned to David's suite in the Warwick where Defries, shirtless and sockless, still picking at breakfast, asks if he knows who to call to arrange a meeting with Andy. Zee says he does, and he can. Defries is pleased. He tells Zee he wants to make Andy a pitch for distribution, market him like a rock'n'roll star, take him on tour with David and have him design his record covers, just like Andy's already done for the Stones' *Sticky Fingers*, and T-shirts, and posters, and, well, *everything*.

David is just as excited at the prospect of meeting the man behind his song. He feels he already knows him – everything he's learned from asking those who do, Ultra Violet, Zee, Lou, everything he's been reading for years in magazines and books, like the one his old friend Mike the postman lent him, everything he's heard in The Velvet Underground, everything he saw in *Pork*. And when Andy hears his song, he'll realise just how alike they are. Like Lou, like Iggy, this could be yet another beginning of a beautiful friendship.

New York spits, laughs and gees him on.

BLACK FEDORA PIVOTED TO KILL, David steps out of the elevator, his yellow shoes – now he remembers, the ones Marc gave him on a beneficent whim, don't ask when, with semi-wedge heels and an instep strap Americans call 'Mary Janes' – clattering on the hardwood floor of a large white reception area. A couple of photos hang on walls, barely breaking up the overwhelming shock of plain white. It's not the silvery warehouse David imagined, but then Andy's Factory isn't the same Midtown Factory where The Velvet Underground rehearsed and where Marilyns and Brillos were screenprinted on the concrete floor. Now it's on the sixth storey of a thin arabesque block on Union Square. Clean and minimal, not a stray speck of paint underfoot: more like an office, with a screening room in the back, and less easy to drop in and hang out after Andy was shot here three years ago. There's also a 'guard dog': a spotted Great Dane – stuffed. It's Andy's joke. He calls it 'Cecil' since he swears it used to belong to Cecil B. DeMille. This, too, may be one of Andy's jokes.

The backroom door opens. Not Andy, not yet, but his director, Paul Morrissey. David and Defries wait expectantly. And then he appears.

He looks so like Andy it's like staring at a cut-out, as if his whole body has been screenprinted and stuck in a perfect Andy-shaped hole in space. Dressed soberly in shirt and slacks, the dyed white fringe flopping over dark glasses, the mouth set to a permanent half-open 'uh'. Just as Zee had described.

'Uh.'

Which might have been Andy saying 'hi'. A wraithlike hand extends. David shakes it. His fingers feel like they've briefly clutched a cold door handle.

'Uh.'

He's a two-dimensional man navigating a world of three.

'Uh.'

Which is Paul's cue to lead them through to take a seat. Everyone's eyes are on Andy.

'Uh.'

Where Andy's eyes are, nobody can tell behind the shades.

'Uh.'

Defries begins his spiel, about Andy, his films and their distribution in Europe.

'Uh.'

Andy doesn't appear to be listening.

'Uh.'

His head swivels, slow as a murderer creeping up on their victim over squeaky floorboards.

'Uh.'

His shades seem to be pointed at David.

'Uh.'

David's throat feels dry, but he's desperate to speak.

'Uh.'

Just to break the silence of the deafening –

'Uh.'

'I've got a song to play you . . .' says David. 'I . . . a song about you . . . it's going to be on my next album. I've got a copy here.'

'Uh.'

David fumbles in his bag and pulls out the acetate. Paul leads him over to their stereo in the corner. David places it on the turntable, checks the speed, and drops the stylus. The speakers vibrate with the flamenco rhythm of 'Andy Warhol'. David turns around. Andy's seat is empty.

'   '

He's left the room. David stands, squirming, letting the record play. The song finishes. Then Andy reappears.

'Uh.'

He sits back down in his chair.

'Uh,' says the chair.

Nobody says anything.

'Uh.'

David forces it out. 'What did you think?'

'Uh . . .'

Andy's mouth hangs open.

'. . . uh . . .'

The thought finishing.

'. . . I really . . . uh . . . I like your shoes.'

'Oh?'

'Uh.'

Andy suddenly produces a Polaroid camera. He points it at David. A button is pressed. The camera makes a slow, mechanical noise and shoots out an undeveloped print. The noise is like a robot saying 'uh'.

Andy places the photo on the coffee table in front of him.

'Uh.'

He takes another.

'Uh.'

Over in the corner of the studio sits a strange-looking trolley with a mounted heavy-duty video camera. It's there for Andy's helpers to keep a visual diary of Factory guests. David is invited to record a little memento of his visit and accepts, relieved to have something to do other than wait for the next –

'Uh.'

So is Defries.

'Uh.'

David instructs the camera operator to zoom out so his whole body can be seen in frame. His fedora stays on, his hair drooping down over a tight rollneck sweater above high-waisted Oxford bags.

'Uh.'

David puts his hand in his trouser pocket then pulls it out pretending it's now holding a pair of invisible scissors. He mimes cutting his chest open from navel to collar bone.

'Uh.'

He places the 'scissors' back in his pocket. He pretends to put his hands inside his body, grabbing his intestines, pulling them out like a firehose, one hand over the other, until they reach the end.

'Uh.'

Still holding tight, he pulls out his 'scissors' again. He snips off the last bit of his pretend intestines.

'Uh.'

Defries has edged towards the exit, anxiously clawing his afro in the hope that if he scratches his scalp hard enough, he'll wake up and find none of this is happening.

Andy, immobile, stands watching David.

'Uh.'

David pushes his hands together in a downward V, tip to tip, flicking his thumbs in unison so it looks like the top of a beating heart. He raises it up in front of him and throws it in the air, like releasing a pigeon.

'Uh.'

The mimes refuse to stop.

David trapped behind a pane of glass.

'Uh.'

David stuck in a tube.

'Uh.'

David flapping his arms like a birdie.

'Uh.'

But the hour is already lost. When Defries makes their excuses to leave, nobody begs them to stay.

'Uh.'

The last thing David sees before the elevator doors slide shut is Cecil the Great Dane, standing alert, pointy ears erect, fixing him with its dead glassy eyes. Like a silent, stuffed, parting 'uh'.

UNHURRIED STEPS carry Andy back over David's invisible guts to the coffee table where the Polaroids he took lie face up, now fully developed. He bends down, his lips twisting the thinnest of smiles. He picks one up, cheeks dimpling. 'Yeah,' he nods, his voice suddenly clear. 'Really nice shoes.'

TWENTY

ENOUGH! ENOUGH FILTH! ENOUGH SMUT! Enough pollution of the mind and spirit. Enough of *Oz* magazine, and naked Shakespeare on the stage, and sex education films for school children. Enough of Jagger's buttocks in *Performance*, and fellatio in Warhol's *Flesh*, and Ken Russell's *The Devils*, which the Vatican in all their papal propriety ban as 'the most obscene thing we've ever seen on screen!' Enough of Swedish films, and strip clubs, and the tabloids' corrupting contours of Valerie Leon, Vicki Hodge and, minx of minxes, Caroline Munro. Enough of foul language on licence-payers' screens and the saucy witchcraft of Pan's People. Enough of explicit nipples on bra adverts displayed in underground stations and praise be to London Transport for painting them out. Enough of the plague of permissiveness poisoning British youth, in dress, in haircut, in premarital copulating damnation. Enough of abortion, and contraception, and Wimpy burgers after midnight, and all perverted Jezebels who dare blaspheme against the scullery floor the Good Lord has provided for them. Enough of their vices of cloth, the abominable French trend for 'false feller' suits as women shun their aprons for pinstripes, cravats and ties which even the *TV Times* refer to – without shame! – as this season's 'dykey look'. Enough of that sin of sins, the undiscussable scourge of buggery, and tribadism, and those who promote it as anything other than punishable by eternal hellfire. Enough of their disgraceful marches, and dirty leaflets, and

135

depraved magazines asking: *'Does it offend you as you sit watching* Coronation Street *to think that somewhere two males under 21 are screwing the daylight/moonlight/fuck/ass/cocksuck/want-it-want-it-want-it out of each other as the world outside continues unperturbed?'* Because the answer is YES! ENOUGH IS ENOUGH! And THEY are not going to take any more!

They. Christ's children. Reich of Heaven. Sturmbannführers of decent society committed to cleansing Britain of its moral decay. Torchlit goosesteppers united against the godless darkness. As named – the Festival of Light!

Today is their day. They've been planning it for six months: a mass gathering in central London for prayer, hymns and Christian rejoicing followed by a night of burning beacons and Cliff Richard. They're expecting a crowd of 100,000 – as many as the Weeley Festival – from every pew in the nation. Its headline acts: Lord Longford, a 65-year-old peer who recently undertook an investigative anti-porn holiday to Copenhagen just to stoke his bile with triple Xs; Malcolm Muggeridge, a 68-year-old journalist and contrarian who two weeks ago told a packed Christian meeting in Westminster's Methodist Central Hall, 'I'm afraid I don't like homosexuals'; Mary Whitehouse, the 61-year-old freeze-dried gorgon who sets the Teasmade alarm for 6 a.m. so she can start each day with a hot beverage and a horn-rimmed flick of Holy Scripture; and Cliff himself, now 30, who recently told *Rave* magazine he believes porn films create rapists and 'sex outside marriage is fornication – and that is wrong!' Together, these Four Messerschmitts of the Godpocalypse and their flock will heal the sick of mind, save the lost of soul, and proclaim the word of the Lord: 'Moral pollution needs a solution!' *Hallelujah, abide with me, and we're all going on a summer holiday! Amen!*

But there's a little bear, like you've never seen before, who's a lot more fun. And it's his plan to do to the Festival of Light what he recently did to Mary Whitehouse on the cover of *Ink* magazine. 'Operation Rupert'. A strategic counterattack led by the Gay Liberation Front, who've even planted moles among their enemies' volunteer army of propaganda envelope stuffers. Armed with the where, when, how and who, they've drawn up a battle plan of sabotage and disruption, just as they did at Muggeridge and friends' last meeting in Central Hall: gatecrashing dressed as nuns, can-canning down the aisles, releasing mice, throwing talcum powder, littering seats with pornography hidden in fake religious-looking pamphlets and proudly exhibiting the art of the loud, long, sloppy gay kiss.

The Festival of Light have God and a good luck message from Prince Charles on their side, but not Tony Blackburn, who they asked and who told them bluntly he had 'no sympathy for any of your aims'. Nor, alas, the late September weather. Grey clouds drizzle over Trafalgar Square as the Christian soldiers start to assemble, just after 2 p.m. Many have come from afar by the coachload, and many a coachload has been diverted away by the commandos of Rupert posing as festival traffic wardens. The crowd is smaller than prayed for – only around 35,000 – though much of it alarmingly young: frightening specimens isolated from their age for whom T. Rex is just a cooking oil, bible-bashed-to-braindead drones holding banners reading 'JESUS IS LIGHT' with eyes that have none. The older ones look like people from a photograph taken 30 years earlier, ration-book faces moaning hymns like a burst bagpipe as the rainclouds twirl and the sermons on Nelson's mount begin.

So it shall be written in the Gospel According to Rupert.

And then a voice did pipe up, and it was a loud voice, and it sayeth clear so all the cheerless lambs might hear, 'JESUS WAS GAY!' And the lambs did gasp, and some of them did search for the mouth from whence it came and grumble 'No, he wasn't!' And smoke and stink bombs did burst, and their cloud and odour spread among the congregation, and it was a thick smoke, and a rotten stink. And other banners did raise, and their messages readeth 'ALL GOD'S CHILDREN GOT NIPPLES' and 'GO TO HELL – IT'S MORE FUN', and heathens did parade an open coffin for 'LIBERTY', and strange women did walk chained together in the cloth of 'businessmen and downtrodden housewives', pushing dolls in prams. And four men did appear dressed as nuns, and they did brandish the fruit of the cucumber in a manner that did not make God happy, and they were manhandled by good persons of the law. And verily another malefactor did appear in the guise of Mary Whitehouse, and he did ascend the platform beside the real Mary Whitehouse, and the crowd were confused. And he, too, was thrown into a Black Maria for being so wicked.

And then the thousands did march onwards to Hyde Park where they would be blessed by the prophet named Cliff. And the heathens did follow and did salute the disciples of Whitehouse with stiff arms and demonic hollers of '*Sieg Heil*!' And the righteous crowd did ignore them and sing 'He's Got The Whole World In His Hands'. And the sinners sang along. *'He's got the whole world . . . in his pants.'* And when the prophet did appear the people were joyous, even the evildoers, for they did exclaim 'CLIFF IS GAY!' And the idolater known as Father Fuck of Tooting did distribute among the hairy ones a giant cake containing the crazy herb baked in the shape of a phallus, and those who ate it went inexplicably mad with happiness. And the agents of the police did make many arrests, with or without reason, and when there wasn't a reason they sayeth unto their prisoners, 'We think you lot have connections with the Angry Brigade.' And Operation Rupert was over, and the Festival of Light did wane to a flicker just as *The Des O'Connor Show* was starting. And Des did sing *'Try a little kindness, or you'll overlook the blindness, of the narrow-minded people on the narrow-minded streets.'* And God did shrug 'whatever' and switch over to *Ironside*.

AND AS THE COACHES OF CHRISTIANS kumbaya their way back up the M1 to dream chaste dreams under coal tar-scented sheets, a few hundred unsaved souls in the market town of Aylesbury watch David in metamorphosis. His concert at the Friars Club in the Borough Assembly Hall begins with the same acoustic covers of Biff Rose and Jacques Brel he's been playing for years. He rambles between songs, mimicking *Monty Python*'s 'saynomore!' and spinning stoned word jazz about his American travels like an amateur stand-up. In the audience his paymasters from Gem look on warily, Defries unimpressed, Laurence biting his lip. 'God,' he mutters under his breath. 'This is *awful*.'

A lot of it is. But it is also a necessary goodbye: to Biff bloody Rose; to waffling to every crowd like they're a student folk club; to trying to be *himself* on stage. Goodbye to the unsure busker the world will never have to see again. Hello to the rock'n'roll illusionist. David's hour on stage in Aylesbury is a ritual of transition from one to the other. Song by song, heavier, louder, stronger, balustraded by the force of Mick, Trevor and Woody, his biology changing, the space seedpod splitting, the body snatching, the past shrivelling, the future screaming welcome in Chuck Berry's 'Round And Round' and Lou's 'I'm Waiting For The Man'. Borrowed words and music which in shaking bodies and stomping applause teach him all he needs to know about how – from this day forth – to shape his own. Just look at the kids. It's all they want for their 50p on a Saturday night to keep them away from mum, dad, boredom and Des O'Connor. Sick and dirty crazy sounds that never stop rocking till the moon goes down. You can't stop it. You can't kill it. You can't exorcise it from Trafalgar Square with Jesus banners and the 23rd Psalm. You can't shackle it with a scroll and mortarboard. You can't imprison it because it's always free – and always will be. It's as old as sweet sin and timeless as starlight. It's in Elvis's lips, Little Richard's lashes, Chuck's knees, Gene's limp, Jagger's wrists, Marc's curls, Lou's sneer and Iggy's laugh. It passes from soul to soul like a howling wind seeking out the loudest shells to blow its beautiful call. And tonight, at last, it's found David.

The next date in his diary is a week on Monday. A benefit concert in a swimming baths in Marylebone for the Gay Liberation Front. Their sabres are rattling louder than ever in the aftermath of Operation Rupert, desperate for funds to support their war on bigotry, for pamphlets and demos, and their weekly meetings now at a church hall just round the corner from the *Performance* house on Powis Square. The cause is just and David the star attraction. Until he pulls out only days before – but too late to stop the listing in *Time Out* accompanied by one of his effeminate Garbo-pose portraits.

Without his name to sell the £1 tickets the benefit is cancelled and the GLF left raging. All they're told is that he decided 'it wouldn't look good'. Well, too much risk of people thinking he wants to be a leader. Who, *David*? Oh no, dear. Not *now*. All *he* wants is to be *worshipped*. As a god.

TWENTYONE

THE GODS NO LONGER SPEAK IN BURNING BUSHES. Their tablets are paper, not stone. Thin and smudgy, thick and glossy, 6 new pence or 25, their commandments cheap and 20 to the dozen.

'DAVID!'

No, not that David. A different god. Many months ago, he crept to number 18 in the charts with his American TV family – *The Partridge Family* – and a song like a Jewish wedding dance called 'I Think I Love You'. That was before the Partridges nested on British screens. Now they have. *'Shirley and her five music-crazy children'* are on BBC One every Saturday teatime before *The Generation Game*, setting gymslips flapping for David Cassidy. As his every disciple knows, he is 5 feet 8 inches, weighs 125 lbs, likes the colour brown, eating lobster and listening to Creedence Clearwater Revival. David lives in Hollywood and has yet to set foot on British soil. 'One of these days I'm going to do the one thing I've always wanted to do,' he promises UK fans in his new column for *Fabulous 208*. 'Hop on a plane and come and see all of you in person.' Loudly do the poster-kissing lips pray for that moment.

The same young lips do not yet pray to David Bowie, though his testaments, old and new, are all out there for those who seek them.

'I'm not a transvestite. I wear *men's* dresses. I wear butch gay clothes.'

So would you like to be a star, David?

'Yes.'

But you wouldn't like the responsibility?

'No.'

So what are you going to do about it?

'Get fucked up probably!'

What do you think of rock music today?

'I feel we're all in a fucking dead industry that relates to nothing anymore. Our music has lost its validity.'

Isn't there any good music around?

'Good music doesn't interest me. The most important person in Europe and England today is Marc Bolan, not because of what he says but because he is the first person who has latched onto the energy of the young once again. He has got his dictatorships fixed up. He has that star quality. That is very important. Marc Bolan is the new angry young man. Marc Bolan has that angry young life. You can quote me on that. I also like Iggy Stooge and the Flamin' Groovies. Rock should tart itself up a bit more, you know. People are scared of prostitution. There should be some real unabashed prostitution in this business.'

Meanwhile, in another parish, the most important person in England today discusses unabashed prostitution.

'I'll go up now and kiss guys if I think they're nice. It doesn't mean I'm homosexual.'

So why do you camp it up on Top of the Pops, *Marc?*

'Oh, come on! I've always been a wriggler. I just dig dancing. I mean I *am* my own fantasy. I am the "Cosmic Dancer" who dances his way out of the womb and into the tomb. I'm not frightened to get up there and groove about in front of six million people on TV because it doesn't look cool. That's the way I would do it at home. It's not serious. I'm serious about the music, but I'm not serious about the fantasy.'

Meanwhile, in another street in another town, a pillar box swallows felt-tip sacrilege.

'Marc Bolan is not, by any stretch of the imagination, a crucial figure in the world of contemporary music. For sanity's sake, leave him alone before he starts to imagine that he is important.'

And so a big nobody from Kent becomes a small somebody in the letters page of *Melody Maker*.

Meanwhile, John Lennon blames it all on the Nazis.

'If it wasn't for Goebbels, you wouldn't have *Melody Maker* and its adverts, and you survive by adverts.'

The man whose new single imagines a world with nothing to kill or die for, who was last seen clicking his heels through the streets of London holding a copy of a revolutionary Marxist newspaper supporting the IRA, has a poke at the *Maker*. The *Maker* pokes back.

But Goebbels didn't invent adverts?

'Yeah,' says Lennon, 'but Goebbels finalised it to a fantastic art form. All modern advertising came from Goebbels. I mean, I'm not saying he's a hero. I'm just telling you what he did.'

Meanwhile, back in Beckenham, David, too, is talking a load of old Goebbels.

'Dictatorships are fine.'

Pardon, David?

'Much better than a stupid committee of 18 or 19 people. I wouldn't mind Mao here in this country. As the Earth has probably only another 40 years of existence, this would be a fine time to have a dictatorship.'

But why?

'I'm fed up with being free. I can't do anything with it. I like being dictated to because I'm not so clever anyway. I'd much rather feel that I'm being repressed. At least then you have something to live for.'

And meanwhile, over in California, with nothing to live for, the pickled varicose flesh of Gene Vincent – who will never sing 'Hang On To Yourself', who has no self left to hang on to – surrenders to fate. Drape and drainpipe tears brothel-creep past Goebbels' ghost to another *Maker* mailbag.

'One of the great ones is dead. One of the true originals, an innovator. Unsung and unheralded. Gene Vincent, the man whose song "Be-Bop-A-Lula" became the cornerstone of an era is no longer with us. But we shall remember Gene Vincent, not as the fallen idol, but as he was in The Girl Can't Help It, *as he was when he toured with Cochran. We shall remember him as the great rock'n'roller.'*

The letter is signed.

'Shakin' Stevens.'

★

THE BODY DIES AND THE SPIRIT PASSES. All the life energy vibrating the atoms must go somewhere. It isn't Heaven, or Hell. A few weeks ago, the lungs of Eugene Vincent Craddock could still blow lusty siroccos about the gal in the red blue jeans. Now they're flat slime in a cadaver in a casket in the earth of a Los Angeles County cemetery. Where does the wind go? Where does the voice go? Where does the breath puppeteering the flesh go when the puppet show is over?

The day they bury Gene Vincent, David is below ground over 5,000 miles away. Above him, a shop selling spark plugs, brake pads and other car parts. A place where men come to buy the things they need to repair and remodel, not so different from David and his three Hull mechanics who have come here, the arse of Greenwich, to fix, buff, oil and shine up the songs that will make David a god and his mechanics something like angels. Among them 'Hang On To Yourself': the song Gene Vincent might be singing if he wasn't three days dead and rotting a few hundred feet from State Route 14, the song David already sang with the Arnold Corns when it skipped and skiffled. But now Mick's meteor fingers are on it, and Trevor's sinews, and Woody's muscle, and David's revised ramjet sexspeak about tigers on Vaseline. Now it flies and firecracks. So does 'Moonage Daydream', which no longer sounds *of* this Earth but out of it, where it belongs, ricocheting between the stars. A sound David's been playing with ever since 'Queen Bitch', in the key of Lou and *Loaded*, the pitch of Iggy and *Funhouse*, the frequency of the Groovies' *Teenage Head*. Marc might call it cosmic rock, but, as yet, it has no name. Space rock'n'roll. *Star Trek* in a leather jacket. 'Be-Bop-A-Lula' at warp factor five. Planet Earth has yet to hear *Hunky Dory* – not in the shops for another two months – but David is already a light year into the future.

A lightless year and four heavy hearts in the past, the corpse of the 'Velvet Underground' lugs onto the London stage. They are even less of a 'Velvet Underground' than the one David saw nine months ago in New York. Guitarist Sterling Morrison has gone, leaving drummer Moe Tucker the last original member behind Doug Yule and two hapless galley slaves. The group – the *real* group – have never been more popular in Britain: the reviews for *Loaded* earlier in the year were evangelical, as are the current write-ups for new reissues of their first three albums: '*they're too beautiful,*' froths *Melody Maker*, '*too damn important, to remain the property of a handful of converts.'* Inevitably, the curious would-be-converts still turn up expecting to see *that* version of the Velvets, with Lou, as David did. And after every show, Doug still has to contend with people believing he's 'Lou', as David did.

'I don't care,' shrugs Doug, 'I let them go away thinking that.'

The critics go away thinking this 'Velvet Underground' are *'a travesty, a masquerade'*. They are not wrong.

So another body dies and the spirit passes. To a Greenwich cellar shaking to The Spiders From Mars.

THERE ONCE WAS ANOTHER GROUP OF SPIDERS. The Spiders from Arizona. Then they moved to Los Angeles and became The Nazz. Until they realised there was another Nazz in Philadelphia, so they changed their name to Alice Cooper and moved to Detroit. Now Alice Cooper, the band, led by Alice Cooper, the man, live in a 40-room mansion in Greenwich. Not the Greenwich where David and his newly named Spiders From Mars are rehearsing, but Greenwich, Connecticut, USA.

Or would be if they weren't on tour in London where Alice, the man, stepped off the plane with a five-foot-long female boa constrictor round his neck. The snake's name is Kachina and she cost him $30. Kachina eats on average three mice a week – alive – and while she's here in London she'll be fed courtesy of a roadie dispatched to the pet department in Harrods. She's also been immortalised on the cover of their new album, aptly named *Killer*, the follow-up to *Love It To Death*. Because Alice Cooper, the band, are as much about killing'n'death as they are rock'n'roll. Go ask Alice.

'I've always wanted to get a flamethrower and just do the whole audience. That would be a great way to end the act. Mass murder – you'd never have to do anything else.'

The audience waiting in the November rain outside the Rainbow Theatre in Finsbury Park to see the first Alice Cooper show on British soil are soggy but ready for incineration. They drip in long before David and his three Spiders, Mick, Trevor and Woody, arrive with Laurence, all succumbing to the professional morbid curiosity of Alice's inescapable bogeyman hype and the chance to peruse an exotic new addition to

London's live landscape. Laurence is already familiar with the Rainbow's Moorish paradise; he grew up over the road where his parents ran a sweet shop, back when it was the Astoria cinema. Saturday morning magic carpet rides through the foyer's marble pillars bracketed in red and gold, past the octagonal fountain and the baroque mirrors into the temple of dreams itself, with its chequerboard walls, great plaster lions and its proscenium mirage of a walled city straight out of *The Arabian Nights*, and the curved ceiling above, a soft twilight blue with actual stars that twinkled like the night sky. And all still here, having withstood the previous three nights' grand reopening as a music venue quaking to The Who.

Tonight, it's Alice's turn to try to shake down the stars that once upon a shilling ticket shone with the godlike glare from Garbo. He springs on stage looking like an uneasy truce between Betty Boop and Munch's *The Scream*, squeezed into a black leotard jumpsuit slashed to the navel, his band a Quality Street tin of glittery shirts and trousers, long hair shaking as they hack into their didgeridon't cover of Rolf Harris's 'Sun Arise'. The stars cling tight and the audience double-check the artist name on their tickets. In the balcony, Mick switches attention back and forth between the Gibson SGs of the two guitarists. Trevor smirks. So does Woody, faintly nodding to the rhythm. Laurence gazes on, bemused yet intrigued. David wiggles a bored little finger in his ear, eyes drifting to the Moorish proscenium.

They drift down again when Kachina the boa constrictor is carried on stage. Alice kisses her as he sings.

'Ooh!' go the audience.

Alice slips the snake down the front of his leotard.

'OOH!'

The snake slides inside his costume, winding through his groin, up the gulley of his U-bend, leaving its tail end flapping out his front like a huge, scaly penis.

'ERR!'

Kachina finally coils free. The audience sighs. Alice gleefully exchanges her for his next prop: a sword, which he begins fencing at his band until, after much pantomime gnashing and wailing, a nurse wanders out of the wings and leads him off stage.

The audience wait.

Alice bounces back, teeth grinding, trussed up in a straitjacket.

'*I GOTTA GET OUT!*' he screams. Drums spasm and ugly guitars nee-naw. He thrashes, he fidgets, he wriggles free.

'WOO!'

The stage darkens. The lights return and here's Alice now carrying a spear. He gurns an arsenal of needlessly horrible expressions then snaps it over his knee.

'Oh?'

At the back of the stage, a mannequin appears wired up to an electric chair. Alice creeps over and starts beating the dummy senseless with a hammer. Then chucks it on the floor.

'ALL RIGHT!'

Now Alice plonks himself down in the chair instead. Lights flash and drums bang. He jerks about like he's being zapped with 2,000 volts. He slumps forward. The flashes and bangs stop. Alice is dead!

'AAGH!'

No, wait! He's back again! Trying to hypnotise himself with a watch and chain! Which he throws on the floor! And stamps on!

'OOOOOH!'

And now he's got something else! Jesus Christ! IT'S A PILLOW!

'AIYEE!'

And he's ripping it up!

'WOOHOO!'

There's feathers!

'EEEP!'

Feathers spilling everywhere!

'URFFF!'

More feathers falling from the ceiling onto the crowd!

'FFUFFUFF!''

It's feathergeddon!!!

'OOGAGA!'

And, well, that seems to be about all, folks!

'. . . *awwww* . . .'

Except it isn't!

'YAY!'

Because now he's back, chucking out free posters into the front rows!

'RFFUFFAFFA!'

And waving a sword spiked with paper money!

'MMUMMUH!'

Now he's hurling the money into the crowd!

'SCRIBBABBAB!'

It's wild! It's madness! It's . . .

Awful, thinks David, shaking his head on his way out. Alice neither excites nor shocks him. *Look at him, poor dear, with his red eyes sticking out and his temples straining. He tries so* hard *to be outrageous! And it's all so premeditated. All very demeaning. And the* music! *Oh, move over Miss C, it's* . . .

'Very sensational, isn't it?'

David turns to see Laurence beside him, chuckling beneath his moustache. 'As a production, I mean. As a *show*, don't you think? That's the sort of thing you should probably think about doing.'

Mick, Trevor and Woody hover close by, waiting to hear his answer. Laurence's eyebrows twitch expectantly upwards. David whips them down again.

'Oh, *God*, no!'

Laurence reels back an inch. The Spiders smile on proudly.

'No, no, no,' tuts David. 'I can do a hell of a lot better than *that*.'

TWENTY**TWO**

INDIGNANCE KICKS THE NEEDLE INTO RED. The clear-eyed Monday morning after Alice, David and his Spiders scorch the wires in Trident Studios. Music urgent with colour and sex, hot as magma, slick as lip gloss, concrete rock and jungle roll, streetside stories about sucking and fucking, stars and stardom, madness and loneliness, universal love and the end of humanity, rifling Kerouac and riffing Chuck Berry. A private world balling in its own space and time, entirely cut off from the one above still carrying on like it's 1971 when, down here, 1972 already started the moment magnetic tape reels turned to catch David singing about a cosmic messiah.

A week from now, they will have finished enough songs for his next album. Half of them won't make it: 'Sweet Head', 'Looking For A Friend', 'Shadow Man', 'Velvet Goldmine', a new necromanced 'Holy Holy', Chuck's 'Round And Round' and – because even though it doesn't fit, he refuses to let it go – Brel's 'Port Of Amsterdam'. But the other half will: 'Five Years', 'Star', 'Soul Love', 'Moonage Daydream', 'Hang On To Yourself', 'Lady Stardust' and the one about his cosmic messiah – 'Ziggy Stardust'.

Just as also, a week from now, a pub in Stockwell, South London, called the Plough, not 400 yards from the house on Stansfield Road where David was born, will play host to the jazz band of a 'Ziggy Ludwigsen'.

Why Ziggy? Why there? Why then?

For the same reason blobs of dust and clouds of gas collide in the unquantifiable cosmic emptiness to form planets over billions of years capable of one day supporting life. No reason. Just another one of God's little jokes to fool people who really like the idea into thinking He actually exists.

OH, BUT HE DOES! In Newcastle, where he's forced to escape the City Hall in an ambulance lest his uncontrollable worshippers tear his sacred flesh to shreds. In Birmingham, where his conga player leaves a glass on the stage only for it to be smashed to pieces by more apostles wrestling over holy relics. In Wigan, where the manager of the ABC stops the show halfway through until police reinforcements arrive to control the feverish throng. In Liverpool, where his stage is stormed again by mad myrmidons half crushed by toppling lights and speaker cabinets. Wherever he moves in ways mysterious, robed in satin driving kids delirious. In face, in voice, in hair, in cloth, in the few weeks that remain of 1971 there is no other god but Marc.

The last T. Rex tour of the year sweeps through the land like a biblical reckoning, reducing theatres to a *Jackie* readers' equivalent of *The Devils* as young girls thrash themselves cockeyed at the prospect of His laserbeamed glare somehow picking them out all the way back in Row U Seat 17. *Jackie* themselves are so overwhelmed by the tonnage of mail threatening mass suicide if they don't print another Marc photo, they take the, for them, unprecedented step of giving him a double-page pin-up all to himself: which may or may not make him bigger than Jesus, but in the pagination of *Jackie* it does make him bigger than Cliff's ever been. So big, he's just signed a new deal with Cliff's bosses at EMI who, as of the next T. Rex single, are giving him his own bespoke label. As befits him, a class of his own.

Marc can measure it in sales of *Electric Warrior*, ever closer to the top of the album charts where it will soon spend Christmas after jousting off Led Zeppelin's fourth. Just a pity he can't quite double it with his current single, 'Jeepster', a jaguar's whisker from being his third number 1 but for the country's love of Slade. 'Coz I Luv You' is their sonic punch-up between an ironworks and a gypsy caravan, which in its illiterate jig scores sweet revenge for slow kids at the back of the class everywhere. The Black Country yobbos have just very proudly and very publicly turned down a reported 'million-dollar offer' from an American network for their own *Monkees*-style TV series. This, their first UK number 1, vindicates the snub. Slade will always be more Henry Cooper than Alice Cooper and it's here, in the Thursday night trenches of *Top of the Pops*, where their bovver boots belong. If Marc's to be believed, they're going to need them.

'I haven't started yet,' he predicts, blinded by the brightness of his future – all those Fellini films he keeps promising to make, the poetry, the books and that elusive cosmic messiah blockbuster. 'I haven't even got into it. 1972 is going to be a heavy boogie.'

But it's not easy being God at number 2 when you know you should always be number 1. That's why Marc seeks out words of wisdom from Paul McCartney. 'Watch out,' Paul warns him. 'You're gonna dig it, now, they're gonna rip your pants off, but in two years' time you're gonna hate it.' Paul *knows*. He's a heavy dude, with heavy thumbs, which is why Marc asked him for advice. Paul's had seven years of Beatley heavy boogie. So has John: that's probably why he's now reached the stage of blaming bad reviews in *Melody Maker* on the Third Reich. So has George: that's probably why he's become a bitter bastard ripping off The Chiffons and whinging that 'pop is very boring now' to *Record Mirror*. And so has Ringo: though at least he has the good sense to tell the press 'I think T. Rex are fantastic', which, naturally, makes him the wisest Fab of the Four. But Marc's not even had a full 12 months of it yet. And though he doesn't like to admit it, it's already burning him. So goddamn hot that these days he can barely drink enough champagne to douse the flames. Pour him another and listen to him hiss.

'It never stops. The mania. It *never* fucking stops, man. How many number 1 records do you get to be secure, when there's no security? Everyone is paranoid. *Everyone*! From the day they're born to the day they die. Every number 1 you get, the next one that follows you've got to top it or you AIN'T HOT! *Number 2*? To anyone else it's a ginormous record, but to you, man, it's A FLOP! I've got a roomful of silver discs, but if I put a record out and it only gets to number 5 – which is a big record – to me, man, it hasn't made it. *I'm fucking giving up, y'know?* So what you do in the end, you don't listen to radio, you don't look at charts, you *back off*. It's what everybody's done. The Stones, The Beatles, Dylan, and it's slowly what I'm doing. Everyone's scared, man. *Everyone! Where's the security? Where? . . . and . . . hey . . . WHERE'S THE FUCKING CHAMPAGNE?'*

THE CHAMPAGNE FLOWS in Kensington, bubbling to the syncopated beat, glass stems making pretty kaleidoscopes of the reflected lights from the dancefloor. Shiny new boots descend to the foot of the stairs where a cigarette holder waves at their wearer with a welcome flourish. *'Dha-rrr-ling!'* Amadeo, always glad to see his regulars, especially after all that recent trouble with the dykes from the Gateways who came here starting a catfight. The boots pass on to the threshold podium, waiting for snap judgement of the prefects of pose – *Ooh! What's* she *done to her riah? Very butch!* – then stride unrushed to their usual booth.

'Champagne, Juanito!'

So David does *have ears.* Wendy laughs to herself, skipping to his booth in a Mr Freedom bow back dress and matching knickers that make her look, as intended, like Shirley Temple. She's never really noticed them before, not when hidden beneath his lady locks. But now he's had most of it chopped – still long at the back, with bangs at the sides where his ears poke through, but shorter on top, almost like a soft quiff. And dolly new boots too. *Very* nice.

The bottle David ordered arrives with the gratis limp salad he didn't. Angie pours with eyes fizzing faster than the glasses, sliding the first over to Freddie. 'OH, *DO* TAKE YOUR EYES OFF DAVID,' she air-raids. 'YOU'LL MAKE ME JEALOUS.' A smile. A clink.

Freddie nods coolly. He has his own ideas for the new David – fabrics, colours, lapels – but then so does David. He's given Freddie drawings of some funny-looking playsuits he'd like him to develop. All part of a conscious transformation masterplan. The holy trinity: first the songs, then the hair, then the trousers. *Hunky Dory* is finally coming out the week before Christmas, but the photos on the front and back cover were taken six months ago. Time enough for fashion to catch up with him: now *Honey* girls are wearing Oxford bags, *19* is selling Dietrich glamour, the *Mirror*'s latching on to 'the dykey look', and even Hammer horror have joined the gender bending with *Dr Jekyll and Sister Hyde*. When the guitarist from Slade starts telling the *NME* his favourite actress is Greta Garbo, it's time to move on.

David's star no longer shines in androgynous images of the past, but the future. It's this Ziggy cat he's been writing about, his rock'n'roll cosmic messiah. His next role. He can picture it all like a prophecy: the hair, the clothes, the boots, and his band too. Ziggy Stardust & The Spiders From Mars. Just like in his song, only they'll play it for real. The lights, the noise, the screams. Escaping city halls in ambulances lest his worshippers tear him to shreds. Managers of ABCs stopping the show halfway through until police reinforcements arrive. Mad myrmidons storming the stage, half crushed by toppling lights and speaker cabinets.

'DAVID?'

It'll be like being God.

'*David?*'

The only performance that makes it all the way.

'DAAAVIIID!'

Angie is standing, arm outstretched, offering her hand.

'COME ON!'

David blinks back to the present, looking around him. Their booth has emptied. Aretha's 'Spanish Harlem' beckons dreamily. He takes Angie's hand, pulling himself up, liquid hips leading her to the dancefloor. Where Wendy gleams, and Freddie glimmers, and little Daniella glows, and Angie is glistening, and David, smiling, imagines the envious eyes of the whole universe bearing down upon them. And turns his best profile towards the stars as if they actually are.

BOWIE**DISCOGRAPHY**71

January   **'Holy Holy'**
b/w 'Black Country Rock'
Mercury 6052 049.

April   ***The Man Who Sold The World***
'The Width Of A Circle', 'All The Madmen', 'Black Country
Rock', 'After All' / 'Running Gun Blues', 'Saviour Machine',
'She Shook Me Cold', 'The Man Who Sold The World',
'The Supermen'
*Mercury 6338 041. UK version of LP first released with a different
sleeve design in the USA in November 1970.*

May   **THE ARNOLD CORNS**
'Moonage Daydream'
b/w 'Hang On To Yourself'
*B&C CB 149. Both sides written, sung and produced by David, who
also plays piano. In 1972, B&C tried to capitalise on Ziggy-mania by
reissuing 'Hang On To Yourself' as an A-side backed with 'Man In The
Middle', the latter written and sung by Mark Pritchett.*

PETER NOONE
'Oh You Pretty Things'
b/w 'Together Forever'
RAK 114. David wrote and played piano on the A-side (Noone's version omits David's exclamation mark in the title). The single peaked at number 12 in the second week of June.

July   **DAVID BOWIE / DANA GILLESPIE (Gem Promo LP)**
David side: 'Oh! You Pretty Things', 'Eight Line Poem', 'Kooks', 'It Ain't Easy', 'Queen Bitch', 'Quicksand', 'Bombers' / *Dana side:* 'Mother, Don't Be Frightened', 'Andy Warhol', 'Never Knew', 'All Cut Up On You', 'Lavender Hill'
BOWPROMO. Split promotional record not available for resale. David's side featured rough/different mixes of songs intended for Hunky Dory. 500 copies were pressed.

October   **PETER NOONE**
'Walnut Whirl'
b/w 'Right On Mother'
RAK 121. David wrote and played piano on the B-side, which was very nearly the A-side. Disc jockeys flipped between the two, with BBC Radio 1's Jimmy Young opting for David's 'Right On Mother' – perhaps highlighting producer Mickie Most's folly in prioritising 'Walnut Whirl', a peculiar Herbie Flowers/Sandie Shaw co-write on the theme of compulsive eating/fat fetishism which failed to chart.

December   *Hunky Dory*
'Changes', 'Oh! You Pretty Things'–'Eight Line Poem'★, 'Life On Mars?', 'Kooks', 'Quicksand' / 'Fill Your Heart'–'Andy Warhol'★, 'Song For Bob Dylan', 'Queen Bitch', 'The Bewlay Brothers'
RCA Victor, SF 8244. ★Conjoined song pairings sharing the same track bands on original LP.

BOWIESOURCES71

AUTHOR INTERVIEWS in person, by telephone and additional email correspondence with Dai Davies, Dana Gillespie, Rick Kemp, Wendy Kirby, Laurence Myers, Mark Pritchett, Rosalind Russell and Anya Wilson. For extra information and clarifications thanks also to the previous assistance of Angie Bowie Barnett, Tony Visconti, Rick Wakeman and Woody Woodmansey.

The memoirs of Angie Bowie, *Free Spirit* (Mushroom Books, 1981) and *Backstage Passes: Life on the Wild Side with David Bowie* (with Patrick Carr, Putnam, 1993); Bettye Kronstad, *Perfect Day: An Intimate Portrait of Life with Lou Reed* (Jawbone, 2016); Laurence Myers, *Hunky Dory (Who Knew?)* (B&B Books, 2019); Lisa Robinson, *There Goes Gravity: A Life in Rock'n'Roll* (Riverhead Books, 2014); Ken Scott (and Bobby Owsinski), *Abbey Road to Ziggy Stardust: Off the Record with The Beatles, Bowie, Elton & So Much More* (Alfred Music Publishing, 2012); Cherry Vanilla, *Lick Me: How I Became Cherry Vanilla* (Chicago Review Press, 2010); Woody Woodmansey, *Spider from Mars: My Life with Bowie* (Sidgwick & Jackson, 2016); and Tony Zanetta, as detailed in his and Henry Edwards' *Stardust: The David Bowie Story* (McGraw-Hill, 1986).

The chronology of Bowie historian Kevin Cann's *Any Day Now: David Bowie: The London Years 1947–74* (Adelita, 2010).

Other works: Joe Ambrose, *Gimme Danger: The Story of Iggy Pop* (Omnibus, 2004); John Capon, *And Then There Was Light: The Story of the Nationwide Festival of Light* (Lutterworth Press, 1972); Gordon Carr, *The Angry Brigade: A History of Britain's First Urban Guerilla Group* (Victor Gollancz, 1975); Stuart Feather, *Blowing the Lid: Gay Liberation, Sexual Revolution and Radical Queens* (Zero Books, 2016); Jill Gardiner, *From the Closet to the Screen: Women at the Gateways Club, 1945–1985* (Pandora, 2003); Peter & Leni Gillman, *Alias David Bowie* (New English Library, 1987); Gary Glitter (with Lloyd Bradley), *Leader: The Autobiography* (Ebury Press, 1991); Blake Gopnik, *Warhol: A Life as Art* (Allen Lane, 2020); Britt Hagarty, *The Day the World Turned Blue: A Biography of Gene Vincent* (Blandford Press, 1984); Jerry Hopkins, *Bowie* (MacMillan, 1985); Dylan Jones, *David Bowie: A Life* (Windmill Books, 2018); Lesley-Ann Jones, *Hero: David Bowie* (Hodder & Stoughton, 2016) and *Ride a White Swan: The Lives and Death of Marc Bolan* (Hodder & Stoughton, 2012); Ed Kelleher, *David Bowie: A Biography in Words and Pictures* (Sire Books, 1977); Thomas Kiedrowski, *Andy Warhol's New York City: Four Walks, Uptown to Downtown* (The Little Bookroom, 2011); Wendy Leigh, *Bowie: The Biography* (Gallery Books, 2016); Pat Manning, *The Trees and Shrubs of Croydon Road Recreation Ground* (Jenna Books, 2013); Cliff McLenehan, *Marc Bolan: 1947–1977 A Chronology* (Helter Skelter, 2002); Paul Morley, *The Age of Bowie* (Simon & Schuster, 2016); John O'Connell, *Bowie's Books: The Hundred Literary Heroes Who Changed His Life* (Bloomsbury, 2019); Chris O'Leary, *Rebel Rebel: All the Songs of David Bowie from '64 to '76* (Zero Books, 2015); Mark Paytress, *Bolan: The Rise and Fall of a 20th Century Superstar* (Omnibus Press, 2006); Nicholas Pegg, *The Complete David Bowie* (expanded and updated edition) (Titan Books, 2016); Lisa Power, *No Bath But Plenty of Bubbles: An Oral History of the Gay Liberation Front 1970–73* (Cassell, 1995); Ken Sharp, 'The Making of Hunky Dory', feature and song-by-song analysis in *Record Collector* issues 363/364 (Metropolis, 2009); Marc Spitz with Brendan Mullen, *We Got the Neutron Bomb: The Untold Story of L.A. Punk* (Three Rivers Press, 2001); George Tremlett, *The David Bowie Story* (Futura, 1974); Paul Trynka, *Iggy Pop: Open Up and Bleed* (Sphere, 2008) and *Starman: David Bowie: The Definitive Biography* (Sphere, 2012); Ultra Violet, *Famous for 15 Minutes: My Years with Andy Warhol* (Harcourt Brace Jovanovich, 1988); Richie Unterberger, *White Light/White Heat: The Velvet Underground Day-by-Day* (Jawbone, 2009); Aubrey Walter (ed.), *Come Together: The Years of Gay*

Liberation 1970–73 (Gay Men's Press, 1980); Weird & Gilly, *Mick Ronson: The Spider with the Platinum Hair* (Independent Music Press, 2009); Mary Whitehouse, *Who Does She Think She Is?* (New English Library, 1971).

Key period broadcasts and theatrical releases referenced: *The Important Thing Is Love* (ATV, 1971), directed by Robert Kitts, produced by Brigid Segrave; *Mr. Smith Goes to Washington* (Columbia Pictures, 1939), directed by Frank Capra, screenplay by Sidney Buchman and Myles Connolly; *Performance* (Goodtime Enterprises, 1970), directed by Donald Cammell and Nicolas Roeg, written by Donald Cammell.

Period newspapers and magazines. National: *Daily Express, Daily Mail, Daily Mirror, Daily Sketch, Musical Times, News of the World, Nova, The People, Radio Times, The Sun, Sunday Mirror, TV Times, Vogue*. Regional: *Evening News* (London), *Evening Standard* (London), *Hull & Yorkshire Times*.

Pop/rock and teenage: *Beat Instrumental, Cream, Disc and Music Echo, Fabulous 208, Honey, Jackie, Melody Maker, Mirabelle, Music Now, New Musical Express, 19, Record Mirror, Rave, Sounds, ZigZag*; with very special thanks to the archives of Tom Sheehan.

Counterculture/gay and women's lib: *Arena Three, Come Together, Curious, Friends* (as *Frendz* from May '71), *Ink, International Times, Shrew, Time Out*.

American publications: *Billboard, Cashbox, Circus, Creem, Harper's, Interview, Los Angeles Times, New York Times, Record World, Rolling Stone, The Science Teacher, Show, TV Guide, The Village Voice*.

Particular thanks to the very generous research assistance of Lee Scriven, director of the 2015 Freddie Burretti film documentary *Starman: The Man Who Sewed The World*; Tris Penna, producer of the award-winning 2017 BBC Radio 2 documentary *Exploring 'Life On Mars?'*; and to David Johnson, curator of the website shapersofthe80s.com. Also to Mike Scott, for sharing that simple but small affair.

For facilitating and contact assistance, the author is grateful to Emma Baines and Philippa Davies. Also to Melissa Bowling at the Metropolitan Museum of Art, New York City, and Dianne Bennett in Los Angeles.

And special love, thanks, gas and air to the candid childbirth consultants for Chapter 12: Gillian Best, Tricia Darvell, Leesa Reeve-Daniels and my mum.

BOWIEIMAGES71

FRONT COVER

Hunky Dory David (Paperback © Michael Ochs Archives/Getty Images; Hardback special edition © Ron Burton/Mirrorpix).

IMAGES page 1

David, in the shoes Marc Bolan gave him, prepares to disembowel for Andy Warhol, New York City, September 1971 (© The Andy Warhol Foundation for the Visual Arts, Inc./Licensed by DACS/Artimage, London).

IMAGES pages 2–3

Top row (left to right): David, homo-superior, February 1971 (© Earl Leaf/Michael Ochs Archives/Getty Images); Mary Whitehouse, homo-despiser, 1971 (© Central Press/Hulton Archive/Getty Images); Man enough to be a woman, Wayne County in *Pork* (© Jack Mitchell/Getty Images); 'Mandy' enough to be a woman, Dick Emery (© *The Dick Emery Show*, 1971, BBC/AF Archive/Alamy).

Bottom row (left to right): Hot love – a gay disco in a former Downtown New York fire station, June 1971 (© Fred W. McDarrah/Getty Images); The Thin White Duke cut in Ziggy 'red-hot-red' – James Fox patents David's hairstyles for the rest of the Seventies in *Performance* (© Everett Collection, Inc./Alamy); Gay liberation, American style – out and proud in Greenwich Village, New York City, June 1971 (© Yigal Mann/

Pix/Michael Ochs Archives/Getty Images); Gay liberation, English style – London's GLF street theatre troupe made-up to wake up, February 1971 (© Evening Standard/Hulton Archive/Getty Images).

IMAGES pages 4–5
Nuclear family: David, in his Universal Witness bipperty-bopperty hat, Angie and baby Zowie in the rear garden of Haddon Hall (© Ron Burton/Mirrorpix).

IMAGES pages 6–7
Top row (left to right): Putting the Angry Brigade in the shade, Biba patrol, Kensington High Street (© STOCKFOLIO/Alamy); Top tabloid temptress Caroline Munro, in Wigwham wig, models a Kansai Yamamoto interactive 'bleeper' sweater for the *Mirror*, July 1971 (© WATFORD/Mirrorpix); Marc Bolan gets it on backstage at the Weeley Festival, August 1971 – black cherry coat by Alkasura,* Chuck Berry T-shirt by Mr Freedom (© Michael Putland/Getty Images); A 1971 model, swishy in her Mr Freedom satin and tat (© Rolls Press/Popperfoto/Getty Images).
Bottom row (left to right): David's turn to wear his and Angie's shared 'lumberjack' coat as seen on the cover of *Hunky Dory* (© M. Stroud/Daily Express/Hulton Archive/Getty Images); Hot pants – even when knitted, the number 1 dolly fashion of 1971 (© Rolls Press/Popperfoto/Getty Images); Elton John lets his Mr Freedom T-shirt do the talking, backstage at Crystal Palace Bowl, July 1971 (© Michael Putland/Getty Images); The pop stars' pop-art fashion paradise, Mr Freedom, 20 Kensington Church Street, 1971 (© Anthony Howarth/Topfoto).

IMAGES page 8
'RIGHT THEN, WHICH ONE'S DAD?' (© Ron Burton/Mirrorpix).

---

*As mentioned in Chapter 18, Marc wore a different jacket when actually on stage at Weeley.

ENDPAPERS

Keeping up with the Joneses: mother-to-be Angie, David in his Mr Fish dress and their best boy, Freddie Burretti, Haddon Hall, Beckenham, April 1971 (© Peter Stone/Mirrorpix).

Picture research and layout concept by Simon Goddard.

THANKYOU

The fabulous Wendy Kirby, who wore it, danced it,
loved it, lived it and – most importantly – survived it.

Mark Pritchett, last of the Arnold Corns, and all
who shared their memories of David with this author.

Lee Scriven for passing on the precious thread of
Freddie Burretti (1952–2001).

The ace Omnibus odyssey squad of
David Barraclough, Imogen Gordon Clark, David Stock
and Debra Geddes at Great Northern PR.

Alison Rae, the ed with the clearest view, and
Kevin Pocklington at the North Literary Agency.

Tim Burgess for sending good vibes from the Norfolk Broads.

And to Sylv, for bearing with this particular relic of 1971.

DAVID BOWIE
will return in

BOWIE**ODYSSEY**72

COMING 2022